D0850786

Kennikat Press
National University Publications
Literary Criticism Series

General Editor
John E. Becker
Fairleigh Dickinson University

PYNCHON

CREATIVE PARANOIA
in
GRAVITY'S RAINBOW

MARK RICHARD SIEGEL

National University Publications
KENNIKAT PRESS   //   1978
Port Washington, N. Y.   //   London

ACKNOWLEDGMENTS

Harcourt Brace Jovanovich, Inc.: T. S. Eliot, "Little Gidding," *Four Quartets.*

From *The Crying of Lot 49* by Thomas Pynchon. Copyright © 1966, 1965 by Thomas Pynchon. Reprinted by permission of J. B. Lippincott Company.

Duino Elegies by Rainer Maria Rilke. Translated from the German by J. B. Leishman and Stephen Spender. Copyright © 1939 by W. W. Norton & Company, Inc. Copyright renewed 1967 by Stephen Spender and J. B. Leishman. Quotations used with the permission of the publisher, W. W. Norton & Company, Inc., New York, New York, 10036.

I and Thou by Martin Buber. Translated by Walter Kaufman. New York: Charles Scribner's Sons, 1970.

Critique, for permission to reprint parts of my own article "Creative Paranoia" and a number of brief excerpts from various other articles.

Manufactured in the United States of America

Published by
Kennikat Press Corp.
Port Washington, N.Y./London

Library of Congress Cataloging in Publication Data

Siegel, Mark Richard
    Pynchon.

    (National university publications) (Literary criticism series)
    Bibliography: p.
    Includes index.
    1. Pynchon, Thomas. Gravity's rainbow. 2. Paranoia in literature.
PS3566.Y55G738   813'.5'4   78-8512
ISBN 0-8046-9213-0

CONTENTS

PREFACE

I set out to write this study because of the great number and variety of people I met who told me, "I was just reading *Gravity's Rainbow*. It's great, but I get the feeling I don't really understand what's going on. I mean, this guy just *dissolves*. . . ." I met these people on playground basketball courts, hitching rides, sitting on barely shaded park benches in Tucson, Arizona. Usually I told them that they really were getting at least part of the message: the world is a wondrous place, and people who are truly open to experience—and you have to be open to read *Gravity's Rainbow*—will probably always get the feeling that they don't quite understand exactly what's going on. We can't know much for sure. We have to perceive open-mindedly and interpret life creatively; perhaps at times conditions will make us a little paranoid—or will make us think we're paranoid when we're not—but we'll try to keep our balance, try to understand; we will hope for mercy, and we'll pray for a chance to be kind to others. We'll do these things, perhaps unconsciously, because something inside of us has felt the fear of dissolution by the force of the winds, has seen the horror of a friend turned to stone by his fear.

This is not to say that we can't know anything; we are living in the age of the Educated Guess. The critic's role is not to restrict the varied responses of readers, but to organize them and to suggest new responses. However, this critic-reader relationship is paradoxical, since many readings of a novel may, in fact, restrict the possibilities for meanings which the novel offers and may prevent the comprehension of the author's work. My first aim in writing this study of *Gravity's Rainbow* is to open the floodgates of meaning for the reader, while at the same time offering a rubber raft to prevent him from being overwhelmed and swept away.

I will point out some sights and try to define the currents of the novel. However, I am well aware that when the critic casts his net (woven, as it must be, by creative paranoia) into the depths of such a work, he is likely to haul up an old shoe or two along with his other squirming treasures.

My second aim, to show the importance of Thomas Pynchon as a novelist, will be accomplished almost incidentally. The reader will see that Pynchon has opened up new areas for artistic examination. The changes he has wrought in the novel's reader-author relationship will, I believe, have far-reaching effects in American literature. A reader's perception of the relationship between character and narrative and reality should be changed for good by this novel. This artistic innovation is not an idiosyncrasy or a limitation of Pynchon's, but reflects concurrent innovations in science and philosophy which have altered contemporary man's conception of his world. Pynchon's influence already seems to be apparent in the work of new writers of considerable talent such as Tom Robbins.

I want to thank Art Kay, John Hollowell, and Ardner Cheshire for their technical assistance on this manuscript. I need to thank my wife Carole for all her love.

Mark Siegel

CREATIVE PARANOIA IN
GRAVITY'S RAINBOW

ABOUT THE AUTHOR

Mark Richard Siegel teaches English literature at Arizona State University. He has authored several articles on Pynchon and one on film and comedy.

1

INTRODUCTION

Gravity's Rainbow has been the subject of controversy, of opinions ranging from fascination to revulsion, since its publication in 1973. This controversy was exemplified by the Pulitzer Prize Committee's final rejection of the novel as obscure and obscene after its unanimous election as the best novel of the year by the committee's own literary advisers. W. T. Lhamon announced that *Gravity's Rainbow* would "change the shape of fiction,"[1] and other reviewers claimed that it could only be measured against *Moby-Dick* and *Ulysses*. The negative criticisms that appeared, while conceding the technical virtues and the creative imagination which the novel displays, generally condemned it as committed to the "easy truth" of apocalyptic nihilism.[2] This controversy is not surprising, since important novels almost always offend the sensibilities of some readers and create problems of comprehension for others.

The critical attention created by this explosion of commentaries has not provided sufficient help for readers who look to criticism for aid in deciphering this complex novel. *Gravity's Rainbow* provides a wealth of materials which, when extracted from the context of the novel as a whole, can be used to support diametrically opposite interpretations of its meaning. Therefore, while scholars such as Edward Mendelson, Joseph Slade, and Lance Ozier have shed some light on Pynchon's sources, on the precision and magnitude of the cultural landscape which Pynchon has created, and on specific but discontinuous aspects of the novel, the absence of any full-length study of the work as an organic whole has perpetuated the critical dissonance in the interpretation of even some of the most basic features of *Gravity's Rainbow*.

I hope to provide such a full-length study here, one which goes beyond the briefer, fragmentary critical accounts that have so far appeared. The whole of *Gravity's Rainbow* can be completely appreciated only as something much greater than the sum of its parts. Pynchon has assembled the mythos of our time, and the result is a novel of apocalypse, not in the limited sense of predicting total annihilation, but in the more meaningful sense of chronicling the chaos from which a new culture may be born. Religious historians such as Mircea Eliade have shown that myth and religion symbolically re-create the creation of the universe, and that the ritual repetition of this cosmogony is generally preceded by a symbolic regression to chaos; the old world must be destroyed so that the new one may replace it.

Although the physical annihilation of the world as we know it is a possibility examined by countless science fiction writers, it is the destruction of the contemporary culture and not that of the whole world which Pynchon seems to be predicting. Therefore, his major concern in *Gravity's Rainbow* is with the patterns of technology and culture which will determine, in conjunction with the physical laws of the universe, what is born out of the chaos into which we have descended. Despite its frequent grimness, this is not a novel of despair, but one of possibility.

PYNCHON'S EARLIER WORK

To some extent Pynchon's earlier work can be seen as a preparation for *Gravity's Rainbow:* Pynchon's short stories and novels all deal with the collapse of culture and the implications of that collapse for individuals. His first nationally published short story, "Mortality and Mercy in Vienna," draws on Shakespeare's *Measure for Measure,* Conrad's *Heart of Darkness,* and T. S. Eliot's *The Waste Land,* all of which deal with the corruption of culture. Pynchon's short story defines the cultural decadence of Washington, D.C., as necessitating a ritual cleansing. Its bizarre climax, in which a berserk Ojibwa Indian who is suffering from culture shock murders a party of decadents, Pynchon labels a eucharistic "miracle." Pynchon's first really accomplished work, a short story called "Entropy," describes both the cultural and the thermodynamic energies of the world as inevitably running down. Entropy, as the second law of thermodynamics, is the tendency of an ordered system—a chemical experiment, an isolated culture, or a universe—to go over into a state of disorder or randomness because of a leveling of energy and a commensurate unavailability of that energy for work. In "Entropy" Pynchon depicts only two alternative modes of response to this breakdown of organization: complete withdrawal from socio-cultural life, or a human attempt at restoring partial order and at making conditions more bearable during the collapse of the culture.

It is from this dead-end vision of entropy that *V.*, Pynchon's first novel, arises. The similarities between Pynchon and the "literature of exhaustion" writers like Barth and Borges have been exaggerated ever since the publication of *V.*, which is an exhaustive study of cultural entropy. Pynchon also examines the literary techniques, such as Conrad's impressionism and Woolf's interior monologue, by which writers have attempted to cope with the absence of shared values created by the collapse of culture. In *V.* images and allusions are manipulated cavalierly, often for the mere game of manipulation. At the same time, Pynchon seems to imply a criticism of this application of metaphor in the character of Herbert Stencil, whose construction of his own "reality" from the barest metaphorical information concerning V. assures the futility of his life. Since critics seem to be in general agreement on the basic interpretation of *V.*, there is little point in discussing it here. But even *V.* is not as closed and hopeless as is usually suggested. Mondaugen, for instance, disgusted by the decadence of the Europeans cloistered at Foppl's, is last seen riding off into the bush behind a Bondel, a member of one of the black races which the Germans in South Africa are trying to exterminate. In *Gravity's Rainbow* we learn that he went to live with the Hereros, where he sought spiritual enlightenment and personal serenity. That Mondaugen achieves only minimal serenity and dubious enlightenment between *V.* and *Gravity's Rainbow*, between the 1920s and the 1940s, is not so much the point as is the mere fact that the very emptiness and decadence of *V.* drives some men not to nihilism, but to a renewed quest for significance. *V.* is both an end and a beginning for Pynchon, and the critics who insist that *Gravity's Rainbow* is merely an expanded "V-too" fail to take into account clear evidence of progression in Pynchon's work.

The Crying of Lot 49 is not merely an application of the process of entropy to contemporary American culture, but an examination of the loopholes in the metaphor itself. ("Maas," the last name of the protagonist, means "loophole" in Dutch.) Oedipa Maas questions the forced parallels between the thermodynamic and the information theory conceptions of entropy, and hopes that the world is not the closed system which John Nefastis and other characters claim it is. Thermodynamic entropy is a measure of the unavailability of a system's energy for conversion into work, and therefore is a measure of the randomness and disorder which consequently occurs in the system. Information theory entropy is a measure of the amount of information about a system that is unavailable for analysis. However, information theory does not concern itself with "order" as structure, as the thermodynamic theory does, but with the quantity of available information about a particular system; here "order" is seen as predictability. The most information is contained in the event which is the most improbable, since the information contained in probable events is already known and predictable. But the most unpredictable event is the most random, and therefore total randomness and disorder provide a maximum of information. By this formula Nefastis may predict that the minimum of entropy (in the information sense) is created by a maximum of entropy (in the thermodynamic sense). Nefastis's lassitude is conveniently justified by his confused and pessimistic application of the concepts of entropy, but Oedipa questions the validity of this mixed metaphor, while Pynchon himself questions the relationship to reality of any metaphor or scientific hypothesis. He implies that all literature and much science are solipsistic to an extent, because all perceptions and therefore all information are relative to the individual perceiver. Goedel's Theorem, to which Pynchon refers in *Gravity's Rainbow*, states that it is impossible to prove that any logical system does not contain contradictions inherent in the theorems derived from that system, because to prove a system correct one must get outside the system.

The relationship of this problem of relativity to literature is exemplified by a painting which Oedipa sees:

In the central painting of a triptych, titled "Bordando el Manto Terrestre," were a number of frail girls with heart-shaped faces, huge eyes, spun-gold hair, prisoners in the top room of a circular tower, embroidering a kind of tapestry which spilled out of the slit windows and into a void, seeking hopelessly to fill the void: for all the other buildings and creatures, all the waves, ships and forests of the earth were contained in this tapestry, and the tapestry was the world.[3]

"Reality" is relative, but, at the same time, one "reality" is not as good as another. Different conceptions of reality obviously result in different courses of action which increase or decrease man's chances for happiness, for pain, and for continued survival. Oedipa's—and Pynchon's—questioning of accepted reality poses a desperate situation. However, it also opens the door to possible solutions by calling into question the inevitability of the present conditions with which we live under the rationalization of "logical expediency." Although the painter and the triptych are both real, it seems likely that Pynchon also wants us to consider the possibility of her name, Remedios Varo, as meaning "various answers." In other words, like Pynchon himself, this artist realizes the relativity of truth and the multiplicity of possible conceptions of reality, but is not driven to nihilism by this condition. (Varo herself seems to have found true freedom and meaning to exist primarily in the artistic—the creative—perception of the world.) Thus, Oedipa is free to continue her search for some pattern of existence other than the one in which she finds herself living, for some way to help herself and others. At the end of the novel we cannot be sure of her failure to find a new pattern for life, as we can be sure of the failure of Stencil and Profane at the end of *V.* Oedipa may yet be crushed by failure, but, unlike Stencil, she clings to her hope in good faith. While the ending of *The Crying of Lot 49* is sinister, it is surely open; Oedipa is awaiting another clue, perhaps meaningful and perhaps not, to the possible existence of an alternative to her present lifestyle. The last sentences of the novel, the last piece of fiction that Pynchon published in the eight years preceding the release of *Gravity's Rainbow*, seem to foreshadow the later work: "Passerine spread his arms in a gesture that seemed to belong to the priesthood of some remote culture; perhaps to a descending angel. The auctioneer cleared his throat. Oedipa settled back to await the crying of lot 49."[4] *Gravity's Rainbow* begins, "A screaming comes across the sky"; these two lines are connected by the opening of Rilke's *Duino Elegies,* "Who, if I cried, would hear me among the angelic orders?"[5] Passerine, named after a songbird, suggests the author himself about to preside over what Eliade calls the Cosmogonic Myth, the sacred history of a race which discloses the eventful creation of the world from chaos, and, consequently, the creation of the principles which govern the cosmic process and human existence.

All of Pynchon's work to date is an examination of our current cultural problems, of their sources and possible resolutions, as well as of the methodology employed in this examination itself. *Gravity's Rainbow* asserts the possible values of metaphor for examining the possible shapes of reality. Which of the possibilities will actually be realized and the precise shape that the future will take are problems which probably cannot be handled conclusively by any novelist of our time, but, in any event, Pynchon does not see the future as completely predetermined. *Gravity's Rainbow* does not pronounce the ultimate fate of mankind. Instead it examines the particular sources of the problems that are set forth in *V.* and *The Crying of Lot 49. Gravity's Rainbow* is what Edward Mendelson calls "an encyclopedic narrative" which "displays the limits and possibilities of action within [our] culture."[6] It is a book of possibilities which seeks to divine the future through an examination of probabilities.

A DESCRIPTION OF *GRAVITY'S RAINBOW*

An analysis of the meaning of any work must necessarily be influenced by the perception of the plot of that work: this truism is especially significant in the case of *Gravity's Rainbow* because the action in the novel is both bewilderingly complex and in places purposely ambiguous. This complexity and ambiguity are due not so much to the perversity of a game-loving author, as sometimes seems to be the case with Barth and Borges, but to the extremely ambitious nature of the work itself. Although pigeonholing Pynchon's novel would not be especially productive, the kind of general description of *Gravity's Rainbow* that Mendelson has attempted is helpful in showing why this novel is so immense:

Gravity's Rainbow seems enormous in all senses of the word, but in fact adheres to a particular set of traditional norms. Its genre, which has fewer than a dozen members, is the encyclopedic narrative, examples of which tend to appear whenever a national culture is in the midst of wrenching changes in its sense of itself. Western Europe and North America have so far produced seven true examples: the *Commedia*, the five books of *Pantagruel, Don Quixote, Faust, Moby-Dick, Ulysses*, and *Gravity's Rainbow*. (There are quite a few mock encyclopedias, notably *Tristram Shandy* and *Gulliver's Travels*, which fail to develop the coherent organization of the genuine article, or to take the central cultural role that true encyclopedic narratives come to occupy.)

The encyclopedic narrative gathers, through liberal use of synecdoche, examples from the full range of a culture's knowledge, and organizes those examples along the stages of a single narrative that displays the limits and possibilities of action within that culture.[7]

In its analysis of our culture *Gravity's Rainbow* is both a satiric and a prophetic novel, but the nature of its prophecy takes into account the multifaceted nature of our reality: it delineates probabilities, lines of technological, economic, and cultural force, and patterns of phenomenological occurrence, rather than proclaiming unequivocally the transcendence or destruction of mankind. Throughout the novel Pynchon emphasizes pattern and probability as opposed to more absolute and static epistemologies. This emphasis represents the language of modern science as opposed to that of the older, mechanistic or positivist science of Newton and Pavlov. As a former scientist, Pynchon is necessarily aware of basic hypotheses about the nature of physical reality. Norbert Wiener pointed out in *Cybernetics* that Newtonian physics, in which the sequence of physical phenomena is completely determined by its past and by the determination of all positions and momenta of the phenomena at any given moment, no longer provides a valid description of the functioning of the universe. Heisenberg showed that physical events, even when considered as a time series, cannot be reduced to an assembly of determinate components of development in time. In modern quantum mechanics the past of a system does not determine the future of that system in any absolute way; instead the past and the present suggest the distribution and perhaps the probability of all possible futures of the system. Contemporary scientists (and philosophers such as A. N. Whitehead) confront the phenomena of the physical world fully aware that all material observations seem to be infinitely reducible; they recognize that there is no available set of information about any system possibly complete enough to allow the accurate prediction of the future of that system absolutely.

In *Gravity's Rainbow* Roger Mexico champions the new conception of reality that encompasses principles of randomness and degree, while Pointsman represents the old binary conceptions of stimulus-response and cause and effect that demand a choice of one or zero for all events. As Annette Kolodny and Daniel Peters have suggested in their discussion of *The Crying of Lot 49,* Pynchon's language, so rich in multiple meanings and suggestiveness, is itself a vehicle for traveling beyond the simplistic binary conception of reality which demands that something be *either* true *or* false.[8] While humans cannot escape the structure of language, Pynchon's language creates an uncertainty of meaning that language itself is structured to deny. In a similar fashion the multiplicity of myths employed in each of his fictions denies the validity of any single myth, yet this multiplicity reinforces the possible validity of all of them. His style accommodates only probability; his narrators, even when omniscient, imply or suggest rather than tell or assert things to the reader. Therefore, Pynchon's "answers" to contemporary problems often suggest faces in shadows, perhaps turned just a little too far away from the reader to make positive identification possible.

Pynchon is in many ways a conventional writer: he employs an omniscient narrator, archetypes, and a picaresque plot. Yet Pynchon employs and recombines these techniques with devices from allegory and film, and his plot and narrative point of view are complex. The story of Tyrone Slothrop, the protagonist of the novel, is in many ways a microcosm of the plight of western civilization in the twentieth century: he was sent into the chaos of post–World War II continental Europe

to be present at his own assembly—perhaps, heavily paranoid voices have whispered, *his time's assembly*—and there ought to be a punch line to it, but there isn't. The plan went wrong. He is being broken down instead, and scattered. His cards [. . .] point only to a long and scuffling future, to mediocrity, [. . .] to no clear happiness or redeeming cataclysm. [*GR* 738][9]

Slothrop, alias Ian Scuffling, alias Max Schlepzig, alias Rocketman, appears
in the last 150 pages of the novel in metaphorical disguise—for instance,
as the hapless leader of the Floundering Four, a parody of comic-book
superheroes—but he has, in fact, been disassembled as a character, can
no longer be seen by his friends, and his physical presence is ignored by
the narrator, who instead reports random passages from Slothrop's fragmented mind. Other characters, such as Roger Mexico, who are essential
to the main theme of the novel but are only tangentially connected
to Slothrop, disappear completely for two- or three-hundred-page stretches.

The "single narrative" to which Mendelson refers actually focuses not
so much upon Slothrop as upon his relationship with the V-2 rocket with
which Germany decimated London in the final years of World War II.
The rocket's function in the novel is similar to that of Dublin in *Ulysses*
and to that of the white whale in *Moby-Dick*—it is the unifying symbol
of the theme (encompassing all the ambiguities of man's goal and man's
achievement), and the quest for it provides the central impetus for the
plot action.

Many sections of the novel have been ignored completely or merely
mentioned in passing by reviewers and critics because they presume that
Gravity's Rainbow is primarily the story of Slothrop himself and only
secondarily concerned with the rocket. That this is not the case is readily
apparent from the complete lack of relevance of many sections of the
novel to Slothrop. For instance, some of the most poignant moments
of the novel arise from the parallel love lives of two couples: Mexico
with Jessica Swanlake, who are united by the war in general and a V-2
blast in particular, and Franz Pökler with his wife Leni and child Ilse.
Pökler is an apolitical German scientist whose affection for his missing
wife and child is used by Lieutenant Weissmann to guarantee his coopera-
tion and silence on the 00000 rocket project, as Pointsman uses Jessica
to secure Mexico's assistance on his experiments. Both Pökler and Mexico
provide important thematic counterpoints to Slothrop; they provide two
additional ways of responding to "Their" presence. However, while their
brief meetings with Slothrop are not without importance for his quest,
their physical proximity to him is so inessential that they could be almost
completely ignored in a plot summary of the quest. Furthermore, when
these characters do meet, Pynchon is not dabbling in Dickensian
coincidence to twist the plot into a conclusion or to unify his story
forcibly. Structure and theme are more closely related, in the sense that
all conceptions of reality—and not merely fictional ones—are metaphor:
we can order perception only by assuming connections between possibly
unrelated phenomena. Pynchon is delightfully self-conscious about
the kind of "authorial paranoia" that requires symmetry and "Kute

Korrespondences" (*GR* 590), and he pointedly violates the narrative continuity of the story line in the last two hundred pages of *Gravity's Rainbow* with countless intrusions and fantasies.

Finally, however, Pynchon's primary method of organizing plot and theme is his use of the "omniscient" narrator as a consciousness that interprets and re-creates experiential reality. The consciousness of the narrator of *Gravity's Ranbow* is the screen on which the action of the novel is flashed as he tries to comprehend the apparent chaos of his time and to create an interpretive historical and cultural overview of it. The only thematic perspective which accounts fully for all the events of *Gravity's Rainbow* is a threefold examination of this problem: first, an examination of the possibilities for personal salvation, in the sense of freedom and of transcendence of the individual's painful and disharmonious existence, as exemplified by Slothrop and Tchitcherine; second, an examination of the socio-cultural movement toward apocalypse, as seen in the history of the rocket and in the political and economic activity of the novel; and third, an attempt at divining what lies in the future both for individuals and for society by examining the available patterns of political, economic, technological, cultural, and psychological lines of force, in the manner of Pointsman, Mexico, and other characters. Many characters are involved in all three aspects of this examination, but success in the private sphere may doom a character's public task, as in the case of Slothrop, or vice versa, as in the case of Enzian.

All of the main strands of the plot contribute to the examination of these questions. Pointsman wants to find out the relationship between Slothrop's erections and the rocket strikes; he wishes to extend his knowledge of the psychological and physical laws that govern the world in order to extend his own ability to survive in it as an individual. Slothrop wants to find out who is following him and, later, how he is connected to the rocket; his fate suggests the interrelationship of societal man's fate and his technology, and in order to escape that technology Slothrop must abandon society. Mexico wants both to maintain his personal life with Jessica and to continue investigating the physical properties of the world through mathematics; his love for Jessica, whatever its chances for survival, is smashed by Pointsman's manipulations—because Pointsman needs Mexico's abilities to divine the shape of the future and places little value on another's personal salvation. Both Blicero, in his firing of the 00000, and Enzian, in his quest for and firing of the 00001, are men of destiny who cast aside their personal lives to speed the collapse of world culture. In this sense they are the opposites of Slothrop and of Tchitcherine, the Russian officer whose personal obsession with killing his half brother Enzian comes to dominate his social mission, which is to collect rocket data for the Soviet Union. Tchitcherine, as both a military officer and a member of a communist state, should be the most societally and the least personally oriented of men, but Pynchon's comparison of the Kirghiz town where Tchitcherine is first seen to an American "western" prototype (*GR* 338) is an indication that real human problems and types are pan-cultural. Finally, many of the characters of the novel fear the control of a "They," of some conspiracy which may or may not be controlling and using the average man for some end of Their own.

The narrator of *Gravity's Rainbow*, who has, after all, constructed all the characters from pieces of history and experience, is most concerned of all with the lines of force to which the characters respond; the further his analysis of these forces progresses, the more he commits himself to believing in an all-controlling Them. (One critic has gone so far as to call *Gravity's Rainbow* "Pynchon's Paranoid History."[10]) First of all, as a narrator he is more or less committed to "seeing connections"; yet his awareness of the possibly arbitrary and artificial connections which the novel-maker's vision by nature imposes on life makes him conscious of the danger of slipping into a kind of "paranoia." Second, while ran-domness rather than determinism seems to be the "law" of nature, patterns seem readily apparent in history, and there is always a danger of slipping into the equally erroneous state of "anti-paranoia," the condi-tion in which "nothing is connected to anything" (*GR* 434). Anti-paranoia clearly seems to misrepresent the physical laws of the universe, which do appear to display pattern and connection, however incomprehensible these may seem at times. The narrator's main problem, both in telling his story and in comprehending the contemporary world from societal and individual perspectives, is to discover the correct laws of interconnection by which to make sense of things without misrepresenting them.

INTERPRETIVE POSITIONS ON *GRAVITY'S RAINBOW*

While almost everyone who has read *Gravity's Rainbow* agrees that it is an analysis of contemporary western culture that attempts to suggest the probable future of that culture, there is very little agreement as to what the analysis actually shows to be the characteristic problems of that culture or their probable outcomes. However, because there is at least this general agreement about what Pynchon is attempting, the forty or so critical interpretations of *Gravity's Rainbow* listed in the bibliography of this study could be placed on a continuum.

At one end of the continuum are those readings of the novel which posit that it is a nihilistic extravaganza whose message is "Death Rules," and whose prediction is the imminent extinction of mankind.[11] The rocket is seen as purely a symbol and agent of death, of man's death wish incarnated by his deadly technology. (The technology in itself may be seen as either life-denying—V. is frequently cited in support of this point—or perverted by man's death wish to serve this end alone.) The title "Gravity's Rainbow" is then seen as ironic: God's promise which the rainbow represents is merely never again to destroy the world by flood, and the rocket represents the fire next time.[12] The only possible "transcendence" or "illumination" that can occur to characters in such a novel would be a vision of death, and these readers therefore see Blicero, to a large extent, as Pynchon's spokesman.

Somewhat more positive, though perhaps less cohesive, readings of the novel see Pynchon as describing a doomed world, but doing so with such concern and vitality that his creative energy goes a long way toward balancing his grim predictions.[13] These readings assume a tension between what Pynchon has "honestly" created and some irrepressible optimism derived from the joy at his own ability to create. While agreeing to a large extent with the accuracy of the nihilistic readings, these readers often note that, in "Entropy" and The Crying of Lot 49, Pynchon's attraction to entropy as a metaphor for the winding-down of human history enabled him to describe a situation of inevitable collapse while allowing for the possibility of individual pockets of life in which the process of entropic breakdown was reversed. (As I have already suggested, this is a highly questionable reading of The Crying of Lot 49 to begin with.) As a title, "Gravity's Rainbow" indicates the natural, inevitable process of death; the life of man, like the life of the rocket, is an ascent which seems to promise transcendence, but which is betrayed by the law of gravity to a final descent. Slothrop and the Counterforce are viewed as the rather feeble positive exceptions to the general rule of death.

No completely optimistic reading of the novel has yet appeared in print, nor is likely to. However, several critics have argued in varying degrees that Pynchon is describing a variety of cultural possibilities ranging from doom to survival and even to transcendence of man's present condition of pain, and that, while these more positive possibilities are not necessarily the most probable outcome of man's next hundred years, Pynchon suggests them in an open-ended fashion which does not establish doom as the only possible future.[14] The readings at this end of the critical continuum claim Pynchon's world view has developed from that expressed in his earlier novels, while also asserting that The Crying of Lot 49 is a potentially positive novel. They note Pynchon's insistence in Gravity's Rainbow on rules of probability and upon acceptance of the unprovable as possibly real. Mexico is their spokesman against Pointsman and, perhaps,

Blicero, Nature and technology are seen to be neutral forces: the rocket may be used, as Pökler's wife Leni points out to him, to kill people, or, as Pökler himself says, "to leave the earth, to transcend" to the stars (GR 400). Slothrop, while not completely admirable, is seen by some of these readers as having transcended his condition of fear and pain by losing his ego. Enzian may be seen as a hero who, through the ritual firing of his rocket, affirms life just as Blicero affirms death; on the other hand, Enzian and Blicero both may be seen as men of destiny seeking some sort of transcendence through apocalypse. Mexico, Prentice, Katje, and the rest of the Counterforce are seen to offer the sociopolitical alternative to submission to death.

My own reading differs in parts from all of those suggested above. However, I will try not merely to make a case for my reading, but to evaluate honestly the materials of the novel from all perspectives. The weakness of the "standard" readings of the novel is basically that they leave too much of what happens in it unexplained. A convincing interpretation must be rooted in the novel's recognition of the ambiguity of reality, an ambiguity to which Pynchon, it seems to me, has always been sensitive. Critics who see Pynchon as being essentially nihilistic must necessarily see most of the things he says as merely ironic, and this predisposition to read irony into a work where the reader can rarely be certain of the degree, if any, to which it is intended is bound to create distortion and prevent a judicious reading of the text. For instance, the first of the four sections of Gravity's Rainbow is entitled "Beyond the Zero" and is accompanied by a quotation from Wernher von Braun: "Nature does not know extinction; all it knows is transformation. Everything science has taught me, and continues to teach me, strengthens my belief in the continuity of our spiritual existence after death" (GR 1). In the novel Pynchon suggests that von Braun, like Pökler, may be using a false idealism of scientific nonpoliticization to obscure the irresponsibility of making V-2s for the Nazis to drop on British civilians. However, von Braun's claim that the benefits of his technology will someday outweigh the harm caused by the V-2s is not completely discredited in the novel unless one is romantically predisposed to see all technology as bad or to reason circularly from the proposition that the world is doomed by man.

Furthermore, this quotation, coming under the title "Beyond the Zero," in a novel full of psychic and extrasensory experiences, must be accepted at least in part at face value. "Beyond the Zero" is quite clearly a reference to the world on the other side of the interface between life and whatever is beyond. It also refers to the negative conditioning beyond the point of behavioral extinction which may be responsible for Slothrop's responses to the rockets, to the dream world beyond consciousness (*GR* 119), and to the "ultraparadoxical" behavioral phenomenon in which a weak stimulus elicits a strong response (*GR* 90)—but none of this indicates that Pynchon's use of von Braun's words must necessarily be ironic and nothing more. In fact, the von Braun quotation lends authority to the acceptance of the possibilities of the unknown which the positivist scientists in the novel, especially Pointsman, find unacceptable, but which Mexico and others present as an attractive position.

It could almost be said that Pynchon is purposely ambiguous about his ambiguity. The single factor that has probably contributed the most to the confusion about what Pynchon is trying to tell the reader is the unusual, shifting stance of the narrator: at times he gives the deceptive appearance of "camera-eye" objectivity (which, like any form of narrative art, is highly selective and therefore not really objective); at other times he appears as a comrade sharing an experience with the reader or jeering at the reader's inability to keep up with him; and sometimes he appears as a hysterical paranoid like many of his characters. Because so much of the novel is recounted either through the filter of a paranoid character, who may possibly be suffering systematized delusions and projecting hostile forces, or through a narrator who falls under the spell of his own story at times (or pretends to, in order to titillate his readers), many critics have attributed to Pynchon, the author, the visions of his characters. This is, of course, one of the oldest pitfalls in reading literature, and, while the danger is made apparent in a novel like *The Good Soldier,* it may trap even perceptive readers, as it often does in *Ulysses.*

It should be noted that Pynchon defines paranoia as "the leading edge of the awareness that *everything is connected*" (*GR* 703), and that this is the condition under which most of modern literature comes to life in the first place: the author relies on the reader to find correspondences between names, colors, or the physical attributes of a character and other invisible qualities of the character, places, and actions, while to do so in "real life" would clearly be an indication of paranoid behavior. In *Totem and Taboo* Freud drew extensive parallels between obsessions and religious rituals, between paranoia and philosophy, and between hysteria and mimetic art. In his study *Allegory: The Theory of a Symbolic Mode,* Angus Fletcher shows how allegorical characters, imagery, causality, action, and thematic structure may all be described by the psychological terms of neurosis. *V.* and *The Crying of Lot 49* deal extensively with the implications that are raised by these psychological analogies for anyone—historian, scientist, detective, or writer—who pretends to interpret reality objectively. "Discovering" patterns in any of these categories presumes that cause-and-effect relationships actually exist and that they can, in fact, be discovered. Pynchon is playfully self-conscious of this fact again in *Gravity's Rainbow*, in which he has carried his sense of this dilemma to new extremes. However, once it is understood that *Gravity's Rainbow* is the narrator's attempt to interpret and reconcile the forces of contemporary life, the novel's ambiguity and the relativity of the various perspectives which the narrator advances suggest a rather obvious reason for the controversy over the novel's interpretation: each critical view has tended to isolate one of the relative points of view in the novel as an objective conception of Pynchon's point of view, while actually each point of view is really a part of an entire spectrum which is the "rainbow" of possibilities encompassed by Pynchon's vision.

An important example of Pynchon's ambiguity which puzzles many people who believe *Gravity's Rainbow* to be open-ended is the very beginning of the novel, which appears to announce, rather unequivocally, the impending apocalypse:

A screaming comes across the sky. It has happened before, but there is nothing to compare it to now.

It is too late. The Evacuation still proceeds, but it's all theater. There are no lights inside the cars. No light anywhere. Above him lift girders as old as an iron queen, and glass somewhere far above that would let the light of day through. But it's night. He's afraid of the way the glass will fall—soon—it will be a spectacle: the fall of a crystal palace. But coming down in total blackout, without one glint of light, only great invisible crashing.

· ·

They have begun to move. They pass in line, out of the main station, out of downtown, and begin pushing into older and more desolate parts of the city. Is this the way out? Faces turn to the windows, but no one dares ask, not out loud. Rain comes down. No, this is not a disentanglement from, but a progressive *knotting into*—they go in under archways, secret entrances of rotted concrete that only looked like loops of an underpass [. . .] a sour smell of rolling-stock absence, of maturing rust, developing through these emptying days brilliant and deep, especially at dawn, with blue shadows to seal its passage, to try to bring events to Absolute Zero. [. . .] The road, which ought to be opening out into a broader highway, instead has been getting narrower, more broken, cornering tighter and tighter until all at once, much too soon, they are under the final arch: brakes grab and spring terribly. It is a judgment from which there is no appeal.

· ·

There is no way out. Lie and wait, lie still and be quiet. Screaming holds across the sky. When it comes, will it come in darkness, or will it bring its own light? Will the light come before or after?

But it is already light. How long has it been light? All this while, light has come percolating in, along with the cold morning air flowing now across his nipples: it has begun to reveal an assortment of drunken wastrels, some in uniform and some not, clutching empty or near empty bottles. [...] All these horizontal here, these comrades in arms, look just as rosy as a bunch of Dutch peasants dreaming of their certain resurrection in the next few minutes. [*GR* 3-5]

Those who would prove the nihilism of the novel by this quotation either stop before "How long has it been light?" or explain this light as the explosion of the rocket. That this light is more literally morning sunlight and that the drunken soldiers are, in fact, "resurrected" a few moments later are, according to these critics, "of course" ironic. Many of the leitmotifs of the novel are present in this opening passage (only partially quoted here): "the fall of a crystal palace" alludes to the demise of Victorian science and values; "a progressive knotting into" and "it's all theater" are phrases which describe the novel itself; "the final arch" refers to one meaning of gravity's rainbow; and so on, for a dozen or so instances. Does not consistency demand, then, that the reader accept at face value the full thematic implications of "It's too late," "The road, which ought to be opening out into a broader highway, instead has been getting narrower, ... It is a judgment from which there is no appeal," and "There is no way out"? Isn't Pynchon saying that there is only one possible future, and that we are all doomed?

The reader would have to come to this conclusion except for the fact that Pynchon himself modifies the question. The opening passage is, we are told, a "bloody awful" nightmare experienced by Pirate Prentice (*GR* 5), the psychic who "takes over" other people's dreams for them. A few pages later we are entertained with the bizarre dream of a minor British diplomat in which a giant adenoid devours London—a fantasy which cannot be accepted by the reader as a literal prediction of the future, nor quite satisfactorily deciphered as a symbol in relation to the rest of the novel, despite its suggested connection to Richard M. (Zhluub) Nixon (*GR* 754) or its implications as a Frankenstein monster of the new technology, perhaps a parallel in this respect to the rocket. One could also suggest that it represents the devouring monster of British colonialism. However, the mere multiplication of these suggestions, none of which seems completely justified by textual evidence, illustrates that Pynchon here, as elsewhere (*GR* 14), is purposely undercutting the reader's attempts to confirm a positivistic fictional world in which choices must be either the one or the zero. Both dreams are told as if they were real by the narrator in the third person speaking from Pirate's mental perspective. The reader cannot, then, accept the first dream as a completely accurate representation of what Pynchon has to say. I do not mean to imply that it tells us nothing about his vision, for even nightmares tell a good deal about one's sense of reality. But because Pynchon is so very aware that his own dreams may be nothing more than nightmares, the reader must also be ready to accept the reversal into musical comedy which occurs after the apocalyptic dream as an equal part of that vision. Even if, in a flash of connecting paranoia, the reader decides that Pirate's first dream, which is not specifically attributed to anyone in the course of the novel, is Pynchon's dream, that perhaps Pirate represents the artist who has a main line into the Jungian collective subconscious of his race (although Pirate does not fulfill this role at other moments), the reader must also be willing to recognize that Pynchon's dreams are not represented as heaven-inspired prophecy—all are dreamed by a "preterite" narrator and many of them obviously belong to drug-induced states—but as the hopes and fears of a very acute, well-informed, but uncertain observer of the contemporary world. The rocket poised above the Orpheus Theatre at the end of the novel recapitulates the one that Pirate imagines hanging over his own skull at the beginning of the novel (*GR* 6-7)—but, it turns out, this first rocket bears not deadly explosives but a message from beyond the horizon.

Gravity's Rainbow embraces many ambiguities in this fashion, and, while the opening dream of apocalypse is perhaps the dominant vision and the one that Pynchon thinks is most likely to be validated by our collective experience in the twenty-first century, the reader is told repeatedly in the novel to remain open to other possibilities, because, as Gödel's Theorem (*GR* 320) and its corollary, Murphy's Law (*GR* 275), indicate, there is always something which one has omitted from consideration, and singularities (reversals in the apparent course of reality) do occur (*GR* 396).

In both fiction-making and life, however, some sense of structure must be imposed on reality in order for human minds to grasp experience and to respond to it. Therefore, one must be able to structure reality and at the same time be aware of the relatively uncertain value of that structure as an interpretive system. "Official" systems of structuring reality may be convenient means for justifying as necessary and expedient the personal interests of those in power, especially if the average person is unaware of the relativity of such systems. One way of responding to Their system is with another system: as Pirate Prentice explains to Mexico,

"Of course a well-developed They-system is necessary—but it's only half the story. For every They there ought to be a We. In our case there is. Creative Paranoia means developing at least as thorough a We-system as a They-system. [. . .]

"[They-systems are] what They and Their hired psychiatrists call 'delusional systems.' Needless to say, 'delusions' are always officially defined. We don't have to worry about questions of real or unreal. They only talk out of expediency. It's the *system* that matters. How the data arrange themselves inside it. Some are consistent, others fall apart." [*GR* 638]

First, some sort of "paranoia," an oversensitivity to patterns, is necessary for the investigation of reality; They are not going to reveal Themselves when it is not to Their advantage to do so, and we must be constantly alert to the possibility of Their presence. Second, we must create a We-system in order to counter Their strategy and to keep our paranoia from devouring us. The We-system, we see in the novel, does not proceed rationally—the weapons employed by Mexico and his friend Pig Bodine are rubber penises and gross remarks—but it appears to function, at least on one level, simply by violating the behavior that They would predict, by creating uncharacteristic patterns within the regimen They have set up—hopefully initiating singularities, interference ("noise" in Their information system), and perhaps revelation from outside the acknowledged system. Ambiguity, not deterministic certainty, is the essential fuel for such Creative Paranoia. "Real" or "unreal" are impossible to know, since They seem to be defining the meaning of our "reality." It is the system, in this case the system of the novel, that matters in allowing man to structure and to respond to the contemporary world.

2

NARRATIVE POINT OF VIEW

The narrative point of view of any novel controls the reader's attention and directs it toward the correct interpretation of theme and plot. *How* the reader knows something often determines the real implications of *what* he knows. For instance, a novel with a first-person narrator is likely to be filled with the reflections and generalizations of that narrator that relate his particular story to the world at large. However, narrators such as Moll Flanders, or Strether in *The Ambassadors,* may not be fully capable of judging this relationship because of their limited abilities and restricted spheres of knowledge. An omniscient narrator may assert complete judgments based on a clear set of values, as the narrator in the Victorian novel frequently does, often speaking directly to the reader in the first person; or he may dissolve completely, never intruding into the narration itself and judging either only implicitly or, like Flaubert, not at all. Whichever one is chosen, it is the narrative point of view which reveals the relationship between the author's fiction and the world of the reader. It is necessary to understand the complexities of Pynchon's narrative point of view in order to make full sense out of *Gravity's Rainbow.*

As Tony Tanner has noted, the contemporary American writer is particularly suspicious of the relationship between art and reality, between his words and the objects they describe. He is unusually aware that thought is controlled and shaped by the preconscious structures of language, and that behavior in most situations is controlled by culturally determined patterns and values.[1] The artist may never be able to surmount the barriers of his own consciousness and confront organic reality itself as it exists separately from the perceiver.

Henry James countered the ultimate subjectivity of experience by eschewing first-person narration and filtering all experience through "the center of intelligence" of the novel, usually a protagonist who is himself presented only in the third person. Thus, the only "reality" presented is a relative one. For Pynchon, who is not interested so much in a character's mental process as he is in the nature of reality outside that process and in the confrontation of reality by the character, the usual conventions of realistic and naturalistic fiction have failed. An author's selection of detail, no matter how it is shown, is obviously a crucial falsification of organic reality. Pynchon is constantly suspicious and self-conscious of this process, and, as I have already indicated, he lets the "game" of fiction be known for what it is in all his novels. This position, which occurs in many contemporary novels, constitutes a new relationship between artist and reader, since the reader now becomes much more conscious of confronting not merely a fictional world but the author himself who stands behind his creation.

THE NARRATOR AS PARTICIPANT IN THE FICTIONAL PROCESS

A cursory reading of *Gravity's Rainbow* will reveal that Pynchon employs an omniscient narrator, and a second reading should be enough to reveal that this particular omniscient narrator is unusual. The narrative is neither totally a first-person recollection nor an objective observation in which the author-narrator effaces himself as far as possible. Instead the narrator in *Gravity's Rainbow* participates quite consciously in a relationship with the reader, speaking to him both explicitly and implicitly in the second person. "You will want cause and effect. All right," the narrator says before extrapolating a connection between two elements of the plot (*GR* 663). In other instances he makes us aware of the fictionalizing process itself: "Is the baby smiling, or is it just gas? Which do you want it to be?" (*GR* 131). The narrator wants his participation in the fictional process to be recognized, because his narrative is an exercise in Creative Paranoia, a conscious construction of possible We- and They-systems. An optimum Creative Paranoid construction must be vivid enough to convince the reader of its possibility, yet undogmatic and hypothetical so that the reader will not be overwhelmed by unintended fatalism.

The implication of this reader-writer relationship is that at certain times the reader becomes less sympathetic with and less concerned for the particular characters and the plot and more involved with the narrator himself and his particular, more thematically oriented concerns. In a sense, the narrator is the only character in the novel: he drifts in and out of the minds of his creatures—humans, animals, and sometimes even personi-fied objects—without the least proprietary transitions, because their consciousnesses are all projections of his own. Pynchon belies the distinc-tion commonly made between "showing" fiction and "telling" fiction by doing both at the same time, violating the pretense of narrative ob-jectivity which "showing" presumably indicates:

> Once upon a time Slothrop cared. No kidding. He thinks he did, anyway. A lot of stuff prior to 1944 is getting blurry now. He can remember the first blitz only as a long spell of good luck. Nothing that Luftwaffe dropped came near him. But this last summer they started in with those buzzbombs. You'd be walking on the street, in bed just dozing off suddenly here comes this farting sound over the rooftops—if it just keeps on, rising to a peak and passing over why that's fine, then it's somebody else's worry . . . but if the engine cuts off, look out Jackson—it's begun its dive, sloshing the fuel aft, away from the engine burner, and you've got 10 seconds to get under something. Well, it wasn't really too bad. After a while you adjusted—found yourself making small bets, a shilling or two, with Tantivy Mucker-Maffick at the next desk, about where the next doodle would hit. . . . [GR 21]

The elusive narrative point of view here is illustrative of the narrator's continual presence in his characters. In this case, it places the reader in Slothrop's mental perspective and suggests that the narrator himself is present as well. Point of view seems to reside in an omniscient narrator at the start of the passage and to shift to Slothrop himself with the change from third-person to second-person pronouns; however, it is impossible ever to be sure, since Pynchon never uses first-person reference for narrative purposes, even when he is obviously in the mind of a character, as in "The Occupation of Mingeborough" sequence (GR 744). This use of second-person pronouns makes the reader constantly aware that he is being told a story by the narrator from the narrator's perspective of placing himself and the reader in the position of each character.

Therefore, Pynchon does not pretend to create a reality that exists separately from his reader's perception of it. In the place of a mimetic "reality," the reader encounters the narrator's mind as it attempts to structure its perceptions of the external world by self-consciously pro-jecting an imaginary, internal world on the screen of the novel. The sprocket holes that separate the sections of Gravity's Rainbow literally suggest the frames of such a film in which the narrator's perspective is the eye of a camera, seeming to record subjectively from the point of view of a character.[2]

PYNCHON'S CHOICE OF NARRATIVE TECHNIQUE

This narrative point of view necessitates a particular narrative style. Naturalism arose from positivist science and philosophy, and Pynchon seems to reject positivism. Positivistic naturalism asserts that the only significant reality is the content of experience, and it presumes that that experience is easily comprehensible. Because of the influence of American Transcendentalists, some works of naturalism also suggest that natural facts are symbols of spiritual facts which, when examined, will reveal their ultimate or spiritual meanings. For Pynchon, man's ability to perceive natural phenomena is itself suspect; therefore, when he employs naturalistic devices, as in the detailed description of Slothrop's desk at the beginning of the novel (*GR* 18), he usually parodies their effects. The "ultimate" positivist meaning of Slothrop's debris pile is essentially that Slothrop is an aggregate of common appetites, not one of which explains his peculiar reactions to the V-2s on the level of naturalistic phenomena. At the same time, Pynchon deploys allusions to shoe polish, puzzles, and women that foreshadow various aspects of the plot and theme on the "unnatural" level of self-conscious art.

The kind of naturalism that attempts to reveal the structure of reality by cataloging the observable phenomena of reality confines itself to the material and linguistic realms. However, since no material phenomenon is completely and objectively observable to any mind, the catalogs of mechanistic naturalism cannot reveal significant universal patterns. Just as Pynchon rejects positivism as the best possible world view, so must he reject mechanistic naturalism as a style of writing.

Nor would stream-of-consciousness be a more appropriate narrative method than naturalism, even if Pynchon's subject were individual consciousness rather than socio-cultural reality. Pynchon is not interested so much in how his characters think as in what they think. Stream-of-consciousness endeavors to recreate accurately a mental process that is only partially conscious to begin with—that is, a process that is by definition not accessible to conscious, structured examination. Therefore, it is not particularly revelatory of what really motivates the characters, as Slothrop's dreams under sodium amytal indicate.

Conrad's style of impressionism, in which external realities are manipulated in order to reveal the obsessions of the characters, is much more appropriate for Pynchon's work. However, in *Gravity's Rainbow* this impressionism is carried to such an extent that there is no longer much difference between the narrator's internal reality and the external reality of the novel's characters. For instance, the narrator compares Slothrop to Tannhäuser (*GR* 299), and later in the novel Slothrop himself makes precisely the same comparison (*GR* 364). The characters and narrative events of this novel are manifestations of the narrator's vision and are presented to the reader as the narrator visualizes them in his mind's eye; he projects his feelings expressionistically at times, abandoning mimesis in order to give a more accurate approximation of his *sense* of reality.

In his first novel, *V.*, Thomas Pynchon subtitles chapter 3 "In which Stencil, a quick-change artist, does eight impersonations." In this chapter Stencil observes that his own quest for "V," for the meaning of our time, could be seen as "a scholarly quest," a "simple-minded, literal pursuit," "espionage," and as history à la Henry Adams:

Herbert Stencil, like small children at certain stages and Henry Adams in the *Education*. . . , always referred to himself in the third person. This helped "Stencil" appear as only one among a repertoire of identities. "Forcible dislocation of personality" was what he called the general technique, which is not exactly the same as "seeing the other fellow's point of view"; for it involved, say, wearing clothes that Stencil wouldn't be caught dead in, eating foods that would have made Stencil gag, living in unfamiliar digs, frequenting bars or cafés of a non-Stencilian character. . . .[3]

Stencil himself does not appear in the story that follows, but creates seven different characters through which narrative action is filtered, described, reconstructed, and analyzed. Each of the seven narrator-characters shows little insight into the actual intrigue he witnesses, although each reveals a good deal about himself. Only the reader, by sharing in all eight perspectives, reaches a general comprehension of what Stencil-the-narrator has envisioned.

The "eighth impersonation" to which the chapter subtitle refers is a moving-picture camera that records a murder without judgment: "The half-crouched body collapses. The face and its masses of white skin loom ever closer. At rest the body is assumed exactly into the space of this vantage" (*V.* 82). While Robbe-Grillet and other contemporary writers have often adopted the "objective" camera style of narration, Pynchon generally seems to employ more traditional modes of narration, such as Stencil's "forcible dislocation of personality," precisely because he is aware that even the apparently objective camera-eye technique presupposes a controlling consciousness which, at the very least, selects the scene to be recorded. Therefore, multiplicity of point of view, while failing to provide anything like an objective comprehension of reality, creates a self-regulating system of possible interpretations of reality without falsifying the interpretive nature of art. Pynchon's narrative technique, especially as it involves cinematic devices, becomes absolutely crucial to the general construction and meaning of *Gravity's Rainbow*.

Pynchon uses a variety of narrative devices from realistic and naturalistic art, but he wants his readers to be aware that no writing, even that which is scrupulously accurate and indefatigable in describing physical detail, can actually convey an objective vision of reality; even film is not really objective. Pynchon's use of cinematic narrative devices does not, like that of other contemporary authors, emphasize the supposed objectivity of photographic reality, but rather emphasizes the limitations of film as a device for capturing organic reality. Not surprisingly, then, his references to film are almost always to essentially fantastic thrillers or to expressionist works.

THE IMPORTANCE OF FILM IN *GRAVITY'S RAINBOW*

Throughout *Gravity's Rainbow* Pynchon establishes visual backgrounds and has his characters walk into them. This technique is hardly revolutionary—some form of mise en scène traditionally precedes the introduction of major characters in fiction as well as in drama—but Pynchon's use of it seems particularly cinematic at times. Often Pynchon implies film "cutting" merely as his chosen structural device: "Back in Berlin, with a terrific thunderstorm blowing over the city. Margherita has brought Slothrop to a rickety wooden house ..." (*GR* 433). At the same time, it could be said that Pynchon imitates film cutting between scenes to suggest immediate, unexplained experience, as in the playfully sinister and mysterious introduction of Pointsman: "Tonight's quarry, whose name will be Vladimir (or Ilya, Sergei, Nikolai, depending on the doctor's whim), slinks carefully toward the cellar entrance" (*GR* 42). The reader cannot, at this point in the narrative, know where he is or what is occurring. Often Pynchon suggests the viewer's or reader's limited access to a character by implying the movement of the character within, or into, or out of an established visual "frame," and he enhances the effect by referring to real or imaginary cameramen recording the action:

In silence, hidden from her, the camera follows as she moves deliberately nowhere longlegged about the rooms, an adolescent wideness and hunching to the shoulders, her hair not bluntly Dutch at all, but secured in a modish upsweep with an old, tarnished silver crown, yesterday's new perm leaving her very blonde hair frozen on top in a hundred vortices, shining through the dark filigree. Widest lens-opening this afternoon, extra tungsten light laid on, this rainiest day in recent memory, rocket explosions

far away to the south and east now and then visiting the maisonette, rattling not the streaming windows but only the doors, in slow three and fourfold shudderings, like poor spirits, desperate for company, asking to be let in, only a moment, a touch. . . .
    [. . .] But she happens to've glanced in just at the instant Osbie opened the echoing oven. The camera records no change in her face, but why does she stand now so immobile at the door? as if the frame were to be stopped and prolonged into just such a lengthwise moment of gold fresh and tarnished innocence microscopically masked, her elbow slightly bent, hand resting against the wall, fingers fanned on the pale orange paper as if she touches her own skin, a pensive touch. . . . [GR 92–93]

Many of the narrative movements can be translated into film terms: "The camera records no change in her face," indicates a searching close-up, held for a moment, to be followed by a full-figure shot, also held for a moment to display and emphasize her immobility, then a tracking close-up down the arm, past the elbow to the hand resting on the wall. But the camera cannot answer precisely the question which the narrator asks: Why does she stand this way?

    The cameraman is pleased at the unexpected effect of so much flowing crepe, particularly when Katje passes before a window and the rainlight coming through changes it for a few brief unshutterings to murky glass, charcoal-saturated, antique and weather-worn, frock, face, hair, hands, slender calves all gone to glass and glazing, for the celluloid instant poised—the translucent guardian of a rainfall shaken through all day by rocket blasts near and far, downward, dark and ruinous behind her the ground which, for the frames' passage, defines her.
    At the images she sees in the mirror Katje also feels a cameraman's pleasure, but knows what he cannot: that inside herself, enclosed in the soignée surfaces of dear fabric and dead cells, she is corruption and ashes, she belongs in a way none of them can guess cruelly to the Oven. . . . [GR 94]

    Pynchon's use of cinematic devices is not arbitrary and has particular importance for his narrative method. Unlike Robbe-Grillet and others of the mimetic, Flaubertian camera-eye school, Pynchon does not pretend that his prose can be as apparently objective as a photograph; the language that he employs to describe Katje's "scene" is anything but flat and objective, and he quite self-consciously remains a writer describing and pondering a photograph. Photographic reality is essentially external and cannot relate psychological reality or abstract universal concepts as easily as can a written medium. Nor is photographic reality "objective" in more than a superficial sense; figures in its two-dimensional plane merely give the illusion of three-dimensionality. These figures remain "the rapid flashing of stills to counterfeit movement" (*GR* 407); they do not exist on a time or a space continuum except as made to order by the hand of an editor. Even two-dimensional visual qualities like texture may be altered, for just as Katje's blond hair is highlighted in this passage, it might be reduced to a shade of gray in a black and white reproduction. Film, like the novel, has its own rhetoric: camera angle and distance from the object, type of lens used, juxtaposition of objects in the same frame or in consecutive frames ("montage"), type and quality of lighting, and a dozen other factors may be manipulated by the filmmaker to determine exactly how the audience will respond to any given sequence. Pynchon is aware of this, and therefore his use of cinematic devices is in perfect correspondence with his self-conscious use of literary techniques to qualify the perceived "reality" he is presenting.

The importance of film in *Gravity's Rainbow* is frequently proclaimed but rarely examined in much depth. The novel itself is concerned in part with the golden age of German film, 1920–33. UFA studios and several films from this period play a part in the novel, including Fritz Lang's *Die Frau in Mond* (1928), in which a romance-type, anarchic master-criminal threatens to destroy the world before a backdrop of the inner workings of a space capsule. (This film, as Pynchon tells us [*GR* 753], also contains the first use of the numerical countdown in science-fiction film history.) Several of the characters in the novel are fictitious German film stars. Film is explored as the most direct expression of the effects of technology on art, and the entire novel is framed as a film being shown in the movie theater of the U.S.A. (Richard M. Zhlubb, manager). Film romance significantly affects the lives of several major characters who try to imitate its conventions and character types, and two pairs of these characters literally conceive offspring as the result of filming and viewing a movie. Finally, there are countless uses of film metaphors, both implicit and explicit, in the novel.

Critics tend to skip over the influence of film on narration and characterization in discussions of *Gravity's Rainbow*, because the cinematic influence on the lives of the characters is much more obvious. However, a frequently noted illustration of this influence can be used to display the implications of film technique for the narration as a whole. This is the life of Franz Pökler and his daughter Ilse, whose conception is "inspired" by a porno-film and who appears for Pökler for only a few days each year:

So it has gone for the six years since. A daughter a year, each one about a year older, each time taking up nearly from scratch. The only continuity has been her name, and Zwölfkinder, and Pökler's love—love something like the persistence of vision, for They have used it to create for him the moving image of a daughter, flashing him only these summertime frames of her, leaving it to him to build the illusion of a single child . . . what would the time scale matter, a 24th of a second or a year? [*GR* 422]

Pynchon calls film and calculus "pornographies of flight" because they break the actuality of movement into an illusion of movement without participation in the real experience itself. To man, the narrator indicates, film and calculus are "reminders of impotence and abstraction" (*GR* 567). Psychology, literature, and philosophy have determined that it is impossible for man to know reality objectively, because he perceives it purely through senses that alter and distort it. Pynchon examines the consequences: our senses themselves are betrayed by our minds into believing that they can perceive an objective, continuous reality, while really they perceive only fragments—isolated frames—of it. Once we have made the initial false assumption that we possess the ability to know organic reality absolutely, we analyze each frame and may begin either to believe, as do Pointsman and many of the German rocket scientists, that what we are scrutinizing is absolute, objective reality; or, like Pökler and the narrator, we may begin to worry obsessively that what we see is not reality at all. Characters such as von Göll, "der Springer," who see reality in cinematic terms, often make judgments based on film values. One example of this is von Göll's willing sacrifice of his faithful friend Närrisch to the Russians so that he can escape himself, on the grounds that he is more important in a movie-plot sense, and that, in a logical film plot, Närrisch would not be killed but merely detained. Slothrop protests,

"But what if they *did* shoot him?"
"No. They weren't supposed to."
"Springer, this ain't the fuckin' *movies* now, come on."
"Not yet. Maybe not quite yet. You'd better enjoy it while you can. Someday, when the film is fast enough, the equipment pocket-size and burdenless and selling at people's prices, the lights and the booms no longer necessary, *then . . . then. . . ." We now come in sight of mythical Rügen off our starboard bow*. Its chalk cliffs are brighter than the sky. There is mist in the firths, and among the green oaks. Along the beaches drift pearl patches of fog.
Our captain, Frau Gnahb, heads into the gReifswalder Bodden [. . . .] [*GR* 527]

Springer's "enjoy it while you can" and the comic-insipid travelogue which follows is a fair indication of what will be lost from life when it is seen only in terms of film.

The narrator and his more paranoid characters worry that they may be bit players in one of Their B movies, that they have no freedom of choice within a pre-scripted universe: "trapped inside Their frame . . . , ass hanging out all over Their Movieola viewer, waiting for Their editorial blade" (GR 694). More importantly, however, film viewing approximates the nature of man's knowledge of the world. As Henri Bergson pointed out in Creative Evolution:

Instead of attaching ourselves to the inner becoming of things, we place ourselves outside them in order to recompose their becoming artificially. . . . Perception, intellection, language so proceed in general. Whether we would think becoming, or express it, or even perceive it, we hardly do anything else than set going a kind of cinematograph inside us. We may therefore sum up what we have been saying in the conclusion that the mechanism of our ordinary knowledge is of a cinematographic kind.[4]

Bergson suggests that this method of perceiving the universe only through intellectual abstraction must be tempered by intuitional perception if man is to understand the true nature of the universe.

Pynchon pays a good deal of attention to German film of the interim period between the two world wars, perhaps because he, like Siegfried Kracauer, sees this film as a significant reflection of the forces that shaped German culture during those crucial years,[5] or perhaps because it demonstrates an approach to presenting the artist's perception of reality that is similar to his own approach. The significant quality of German expressionist film was the power of atmosphere and texture conveyed by lighting, set design, and, most importantly for Pynchon, the innovative use of subjective camera techniques. There were two traditions in German film in the 1920s: the realistic, which was more psychologically oriented than were American films of the time; and the fantasy film, which tended to be mystic, mythic, or pseudoscientific. It is the influence of the fantasy film, in all three of its major forms, which is most apparent in Gravity's Rainbow, but expressionism, whether semirealistic or bizarre, has always involved a projection in concrete, often ritualized or mythicized terms, of inner feelings and qualities, and this is, of course, also true of the narrative method of Gravity's Rainbow. Therefore, expressionism is ideally suited for both allegorical and mythological subjects. Richard Locke, who believes that Gravity's Rainbow is a "dark" work and that Pynchon seems to be "in love, in sexual love with his own death,"[6] sees the cinema of Fritz Lang and "other German movie expressionists" as finding "its apotheosis in Leni Riefensthal's Nazi propaganda film, The Triumph of Will."[7] However, while The Triumph of Will displays devastating mastery of subjective camera technique employed to create a purely associational glorification of Nazism, this film is anything but the "apotheosis" of the expressionist movement, which was concerned generally with subjective individual relationships to reality and which died an early death under Hitler's totalitarian government.

THE USE OF EXPRESSIONISM IN *GRAVITY'S RAINBOW*

In describing German drama and film of the time, Lotte Eisner might well have been describing Pynchon's novel: "The world has become so 'permeated' that, at any one moment, Mind, Spirit, Vision and Ghosts seem to gush forth, exterior facts are continually being transformed into interior elements and psychic events are exteriorized."[8] Pynchon's characters are often stylized or ritualized expressions of inner qualities of the narrator, but they show consistent, comprehensible, and individualized patterns of behavior. Pynchon does not wish the reader to be too caught up in his extremely entertaining characters to judge their behavior. The narrator's frequent asides, musical intrusions, and sick jokes to his reader parallel Brechtian techniques of the "epic theater," which Brecht developed at least in part from expressionism to counter the extreme subjectivity and empathy that often prevented an audience from analyzing the significance of the action.

Pynchon is an artist well aware of the subjectivity of his own perceptions, who plays Wallace Stevens's game of "supreme fiction" with tongue in cheek, and who expects a similar degree of sophistication in his readers. Because of this, all of Pynchon's characters become, to some extent, expressionistic projections of the narrator's subjective reality. But the expressionistic narrative method does not emphasize the fictional or fantastic at the expense of the narrator's ability to communicate information about human beings and their environment. Characters in any novelistic style are, to various degrees, abstractions of some particular facet of reality which the novelist wishes to explore, simply because everything about each character, when he is conceived as a complete human being, will not apply to his role in a fiction. In *Aspects of the Novel* E. M. Forster clearly demonstrated that fictional "reality" is of a kind we can never get in daily life.

Pynchon is well aware of the hypothetical, virtually symbolic nature of our physical sciences. This knowledge reduces even the premise of cause and effect to a subjective level, and the narrator suggests that the scientific methodology of positivism is often no more an objective analysis of reality than is the religious mythology which it has replaced, in many respects, in our culture. Therefore, science and history may be mixed with fantasy and mythology in a legitimate artistic expression in order to obtain a truer vision of reality than could be obtained by purely historical analysis. After all, as Henry Adams discovered, history is just another "pornography of flight" that eludes effective, comprehensive analysis. *Gravity's Rainbow* includes spirits, psychics, and witches who may or may not be intended as more than metaphors for inner states. It is the subjective camera of German film, which reproduces the consciously distorted impressions of the narrator's perceptions, that is most important here. The narrator of *Gravity's Rainbow* continually reminds the reader that everything in the novel is a projection, expressively concretized, of one mind, and that this mind must interpret organic stimuli by the abstracting structures which every mind, consciously and unconsciously, provides. The narrator mocks the reader who "will want cause and effect," yet he himself supplies cause-and-effect relationships throughout the novel.

The apparent necessity for cause-and-effect relationships to create comprehensible narrative structure, and therefore to falsely represent what the artist actually knows of reality, creates certain problems of perspective for the reader that Pynchon handles ironically. His treatment of German expressionist film in *Gravity's Rainbow* displays considerable research—*Die Frau in Mond* (*GR* 753), for instance, is a relatively rare film—and it seems likely that Pynchon is completely conscious of the implications of expressionism for the artist-audience relationship. These implications are foreshadowed by certain "flaws" in the first masterwork of German expressionist film, *The Cabinet of Dr. Caligari* (1920). A young man named Francis tells, in a single protracted flashback, the story of the atrocious murders of innocent people by Dr. Caligari. Caligari has learned the medieval secret of controlling the wills of others and is able to use his subjects to carry out his crimes. The expressionistic sets used to portray the story are well known: crooked streets, houses with sagging and visibly unsupported walls that crazily overhang sidewalks, stairways that twist and turn their ways to nowhere, and artificial shadows painted on the ground and sets that violate the already bizarre lighting. At the end of the film the audience learns that Francis is the inmate of an insane asylum operated by Dr. Caligari. As the story ends, the casual observer is left with the impression of having seen a somewhat sophisticated study of Francis's paranoiac projections. There is, however, an unsettling element which most critics have deemed a flaw in the film's structure: our view of Caligari's asylum at the end of the film is not normalized. The sets and lighting retain their bizarre and sinister characteristics, and therefore cannot be explained completely as Francis's warped subjective vision.

In fact, because there is no assuredly "objective" point of view in

The Cabinet of Dr. Caligari, it is tempting to consider the very Pynchon-esque possibility that Francis may be *either* (a) indeed paranoid about the good doctor who runs the asylum, or (b) the discoverer and victim of a horrifying plot that is invisible to the less sensitive characters in the film. This last interpretation of the film is a possibility because Mayer and Janowitz, the writers of the original screenplay, are reported to have said that they wanted to create a social statement about the average man's relationship to government in which his will is reduced and trans-formed by propaganda and brainwashing to kill at his leader's whim.[9] Cesare, the killer controlled by Caligari, is a somnambulist deprived of all individual will, while Caligari himself kills without motive and in complete defiance of conventional morality, as if society existed as only another expressionistic shadow, an abstract projection of his own mind. Like Pointsman, Caligari wants control for its own sake. For commercial reasons the film's producers changed the ending—which had originally involved Francis's unmasking of Caligari—so that Francis's "anti-social paranoia" about those in power would not alarm the public. The story of the film's production abounds with such Pynchonesque irony, and the final product is really no man's conception; it grew organically out of technology, economic and political pressures, and, perhaps, Their interference. Therefore, it must be interpreted in whatever way is most consistent with the experience of seeing the film itself.

Although the thematic parallels between this last interpretation of Caligari and all three of Pynchon's novels are striking, Pynchon frequently calls attention to the very problem with point of view that the German filmmakers would have been glad to overlook. Literature will always be partly impressionistic, because words must be someone's symbols and abstractions, and film, except perhaps for certain types of animation, cannot help being partly mimetic, because solid objects are an integral part of the photographic medium. Pynchon adopts cinematic devices because his artistic vision depends upon the way in which he examines external reality. The narrator of *Gravity's Rainbow,* unlike Francis, is conscious that his behavior must seem paranoid to the average observer. Yet the characters and action of *Caligari* are powerfully "real" to the viewer despite the logical inconsistency of plot and the apparent un-reality of the sets, lighting, and costumes, because the plot and theme of the film are consistent with a kind of associational reasoning process, and because the visual texture of the film is consistent in its manner of dis-tortion from object to object and from scene to scene. The reality of *Gravity's Rainbow* is consistent in this same way. Henry James's ultimate goal was obviously to produce as complete an illusion of observable, tangible life as possible; the "romance," as opposed to the "novel," was

free to employ "the disconnected and uncontrolled experience."[10] The
distinction that can be made between Jamesian fiction on one hand,
and *The Cabinet of Dr. Caligari* and *Gravity's Rainbow* on the other,
is not one of "real" versus "unreal," but of a kind of artistry that attempts
to reproduce a sense of tangible reality as it would appear to most people
versus one that attempts to reproduce a sense of a personal interpretation
of metaphysical reality.

James often filtered unknowable organic reality through the consciousness of a character and thereby escaped pretending that he had
captured reality conclusively. His device of a central, filtering consciousness in a novel such as *The Ambassadors* almost totally dispenses with
the need for narrative intrusion: the story "tells itself" through the impressions of the central character. Pynchon frequently shows us reality
through the eyes of a character, sometimes in the more "objective"
cinematic fashion of Dos Passos's "camera-eye" sections of *USA*, and
sometimes in a much more subjective, fantastic fashion. As I have already
suggested, either type of vision could be considered expressionistic—and
Pynchon's narrative technique suggests that we should treat both of them
as such. Consider the following passage:

> From overhead, from a German camera-angle, it occurs to Webley
> Silvernail, this lab here is also a maze, i'n't it now ... behaviorists run
> these aisles of tables and consoles just like rats 'n' mice. Reinforcement
> for them is not a pellet of food, but a successful experiment. But who
> watches from above, who notes *their* responses? Who hears the small
> animals in the cages as they mate, or nurse, or communicate through the
> gray quadrilles, or, as now, begin to sing ... come out of their enclosures,
> in fact, grown to Webley Silvernail-size (though none of the lab people
> seem to be noticing) to dance him down the long aisles and metal appara-
> tus, with conga drums and a peppy beat and melody [. . . .]
> They dance in flowing skeins. The rats and mice form circles, curl their
> tails in and out to make chrysanthemum and sunburst patterns, even-
> tually all form into the shape of a single giant mouse, at whose eye Silver-
> nail poses with a smile, arms up in a V, sustaining the last note of the
> song, along with the giant rodent-chorus and orchestra. One of the PWD's
> classic propaganda leaflets these days urges the Volksgrenadier: SETZT
> v-2 EIN!, with a footnote, explaining that "V-2" means to raise both arms
> in "honorable surrender"—more gallows-humor—and telling how to say,
> phonetically, "ei ssörrender." Is Webley's V here for victory, or
> ssörrender? [*GR* 229–30]

Pynchon can attribute this flight of fancy to his character Webley Silver-
nail. Other similar fantasies come directly from the narrator himself, such
as the story of Byron the Bulb, or from undeterminable sources, often possibly the dispersed Slothrop, such as the episodes involving the Floundering

Four. The techniques of realism can be used to transmit to the reader any vision whatsoever without consideration as to the vision's believability. Nor are abnormal characters, such as the schizophrenic Septimus Warren Smith from *Mrs. Dalloway*, essential to obtaining this effect. A similar effect occurs in *Pincher Martin*, where William Golding produces an entire novel from the hallucinations of a rapidly drowning man, and salts his essentially realistic main hallucinatory narrative with symbolic fantasies justified by sunstroke, mirages, thirst, and exposure. Pynchon reintroduces the narrator into his fiction in order to *avoid* the very appearance of the kind of realism for which novelists since Howells and James have striven. Pynchon acknowledges the fact that art is the manipulation of perception, and even when the reader drifts out of the mind of a named character, he is still obviously within the mind of a narrator who is also necessarily a fictional, filtering consciousness. For instance, in *Gravity's Rainbow* the narrator is often characterized by his use of slang, propensity for songs and puns, and a comradely kind of avuncular bigbrother attitude toward his presumably stumbling reader. "Oh me I'm hopeless, a born joker never change, flirting away through the mirrorframe in something green-striped, pantalooned, and ruffled," he says in apology at one point (*GR* 122). When the narrator asks whether Webley's V stands for victory or surrender, it cannot be a question that has occurred to Webley himself. The reader may speculate that Webley has "surrendered" to paranoia or triumphed over Their dull reality with his Busby Berkeley vision, but essentially it is a question being asked by the narrator of the reader and makes sense only in the larger context of the novel's themes.

THE NARRATOR'S COMMITMENT TO REALITY

The narrator is not merely omniscient and omnipresent; in the context of the novel he *is* knowledge and time and space themselves. (The philosophers might say he *is* "being" or "becoming.") This explains the complete lack of transitional links between sentences pronounced by the narrator and those which apparently proceed directly from Slothrop's or some other character's consciousness. We are always seeing reality through the eyes of the narrator and are meant to be aware of that fact. The novel is most clearly connected to the reader's contemporary reality when seen as a real human being's—the narrator's—attempt to structure that reality in a comprehensible way. Therefore, we are also meant to be aware that beyond the narrator there is no promise of an ultimate, objective judgment of narrative events. In *A Tale of a Tub* the reader can be fairly sure of where Swift stands vis-à-vis his paranoid narrator, but this is not necessarily the case with Pynchon's narrator in *Gravity's Rainbow*.

Charles Altieri notes that narrative point of view from Flaubert through the first half of the twentieth century can be perceived as a "dialectic" between "ironic subjectivity" and "withering, nauseating objectivity." The writer does not attempt to explain his subject matter because complete, objective explanation is impossible, and he would appear as partial or as impotent as one of the characters in his fiction. Instead the writer merely presents the metonymic images that constitute our world and records the different subjective responses of his characters. In this way the writer conceals himself and maintains the illusion of objectivity and control. However, Altieri claims, he must also resign himself to a very partial participation in events; he may not commit himself to action or overt judgment; the author is an alien in the world of his own fiction.[11]

Altieri points out that in the metonymic thought on which this modern artistic perspective is based, relationships derive not from comprehensive structural patterns but from connections or associations not causally connected. Romanticism, symbolism, realism, and naturalism are all "metaphoric"—that is, they implicitly hold that the interpretive structures of the mind, philosophic, economic, scientific, or religious, are adequate modes for grasping reality. Metonymy is a reaction to the modern artist's inability to know reality in any conclusive way—and it implicitly denies the full discursive powers of the mind to generalize about and interpret experience. There can be no doubt that Pynchon's narrator is a "postmodern" device in this respect. His language is explicitly moralistic, for instance, when he condemns Slothrop's "betrayal" of his quest, and his attitude toward certain characters such as the "high class vivisectionist" Pointsman (*GR* 37) or the "apple-cheeked" Frau Gnahb (*GR* 492) is implicitly hostile or amiable. At the same time, his morality is somewhat relative to particular circumstances, and he never posits any "rules" of conduct. The narrator does not seem to be much more certain of the nature of reality than are the characters of the novel, except that he is certain that it is not as simple as some of them maintain.

Altieri is concerned that metonymic art will be conducive only to fragmentary, mechanistic conceptions of the world, and that the "spiritual," in terms of both ethical values and intangible patterns of force, will be excluded from consideration. While Pynchon does not offer either an absolute system of metaphysics or a single hypothetical model for the ultimate physical laws of the cosmos, because he cannot rule out the possible validity of many different ones, his metaphysical relativism is not his ultimate world view, but a means of investigating the validity of all the possible world views. He is asserting through his narrative technique that he will commit himself to certain patterns of human behavior, which foster either possibilities for peace or possibilities for transcendence, and will reject others, which foster possibilities for pain and extermination—all without misrepresenting the tenuous, subjective nature of his vision of reality.

In works of realism morality is intrinsic in the actions of the characters in relation to each other and to society. For James, an intelligent and intense representation of reality assured a sound morality. Pynchon ransacks several different types of reality—scientific, mythological, economic, political, and social—for universal principles and in so doing reveals that each moral system is relative to the particular world view from which it arises. Bizarre moral codes such as Kurt Mondaugen's "electro-mysticism" (GR 404) and Miklos Thanatz's "sado-anarchism" (GR 737) abound. The narrator rarely comments explicitly on the validity of any of these relativistic systems, but the individual's tendency to accept any system too uncritically is tied to the desire to accept false prophets like Hitler (GR 403). This situation seems to parallel the narrator's advice that it is essential to find a balance between paranoia and anti-paranoia, between blind faith and skepticism.

Morality is also intrinsic to the action in Gravity's Rainbow, to a degree, because the plot of the novel involves an important quest that fails for a variety of possible reasons: Slothrop's lack of commitment, the overwhelming superiority of his adversaries, or the impossibility of the task itself. Pynchon does not attempt to establish a rigid ethical code against which we can measure Slothrop's performance, but he seems to demand, when judging Slothrop and others, that each human being give what he can, materially and emotionally, to fulfill the legitimate needs of others. However, this single demand is itself more relative than might be expected. "Legitimate need" does not necessarily include the designs of the elect, although They may, in fact, know the only possible course for humanity, while it may extend to mutual forms of sado-masochism, because this seems to be the only means at the disposal of certain people to feel in touch with life. Exactly how much of a code of moral behavior can be distilled from the common principles of the various codes is a question that can only be answered after careful analysis of the novel's themes, metaphors, and plot structure.

While Gravity's Rainbow is concerned directly with questions of moral value, the nature of reality is obscure, and because of this it may be impossible to divine absolute metaphysical constructions from it. Pynchon's use of Wittgenstein in V. ("The world is all the case is")[12] has frequently been misinterpreted to mean that Pynchon, like Wittgenstein in Tractatus Logico-Philosophicus, refuses to consider anything beyond physical and linguistic phenomena. In a sense, their interests are quite similar. Pynchon is always searching for the connections between language and reality, although he sometimes approaches the problem through parody, as he does in the "Shit 'N' Shinola" and "On the Phrase 'Ass Backwards'" sections of *Gravity's Rainbow*. Tchitcherine realizes that the alphabet he has been assigned to teach in Kirghiz is a device to bureaucratize the tribesman, with whom communication is purely a matter of speech, gesture, and touch (*GR* 338). He knows that naming can be an element of demythification that will destroy the Kirghiz culture (*GR* 357). On the other hand, the narrator himself often stresses the power of "The Word," especially as related to the New Gospel of the Rocket:

But just over the embankment, down in the arena, what might that have been just now, waiting in this broken moonlight, camouflage paint from fins to point crazed into jigsaw . . . is it, then, really never to find you again? Not even in your worst times of night, with pencil words on your page only Δt from the things they stand for? And inside the victim is twitching, fingering beads, touching wood, avoiding the Operational Word. [*GR* 510]

In his study of allegory Angus Fletcher discusses the function of "the magic of names" in both allegory and psychological obsession as that of providing functional models for the things that the names represent. The words may be used to represent reality in the shadow world of the mind, and in this way naming a thing becomes tantamount to possessing it in your mind. As Enzian notes, "There may be no gods, but there is a pattern: names by themselves may have no magic, but the *act* of naming, the physical utterance, obeys the pattern" (*GR* 322). Pynchon is constantly searching for connections between words and reality, but also probes beyond this relationship in hopes of establishing, in some small measure, principles of universal value for human life. Pynchon realizes that Wittgenstein's phrase "The world is all the case is" was meant merely to restrict the proper realm of philosophy. Later in *Tractatus* Wittgenstein said: "The sense of the world must lie outside the world. In the world everything is as it is and happens as it does happen: *in* it there is no value. If there is a value that does have value, it must lie outside the whole sphere of what happens and is the case. . . . It must lie outside the world."[13] While for artistic realism, as for philosophy, "the world is all the case is," metaphysics has long been considered, outside of the realistic restriction, a proper subject for art.

ALLEGORICAL ELEMENTS IN *GRAVITY'S RAINBOW*

Pynchon's work tends toward the allegory and the romance in its concern with metaphysics. Any work with a high degree of thematic content is likely to employ allegorical techniques. According to Fletcher, allegory employs "daemonic" characters and agencies that often embody individual concepts and are generally driven by some hidden private force toward destinies controlled by something outside of the characters' own egos. Slothrop is certainly described by these terms to a large degree, as are numerous other characters, major and minor, throughout Pynchon's work. Because allegory is not essentially mimetic and is often discontinuous with "real life," allegorical imagery frequently employs isolated emblems, such as astrological signs (Slothrop's is the tarot Fool), heraldic banners (Slothrop's family heritage is presented emblematically), or some kind of ring or signet that possesses the power to gain obedience from strangers. (In *Gravity's Rainbow* no one seems to possess the "ring," but all are trying to possess either the rocket or the ring of life to which Pynchon refers on numerous occasions.) This emblematic imagery signifies the special universe of the allegory and encapsulates the large-scale concerns of the characters. Because allegorical action imitates theory and idea rather than nature, causality in allegory is likely to appear magical (a feature stressed in *Gravity's Rainbow*). The action is ritualized and, of course, highly symbolic; Pynchon ritualizes his treatment of the rocket and the rocket questers, and seems to parody ritualization in his military and industrial institutions. (The rocket rituals may represent a sacralization and mythologizing process, while the ritualization in bureaucracies is actually what Weber called "rationalization," a demythification process for dehumanizing people by which institutions protect and propagate themselves.)

Finally, the allegorical theme always demonstrates a degree of inner conflict, which Fletcher calls "ambivalence."[14] Allegorical characters are generally either both attracted toward and repelled by their goals, or aided and abetted by diametrically opposed outside forces. Both states represent moral tension in a single psyche. An absolute moral system, such as that established by Spenser in *The Faerie Queene*, is actually a moral dialectic, composed of good and bad doppelgängers, such as Spenser's Una and Duessa. That the protagonist is almost always tempted or tricked away from the correct path if there is to be an interesting plot, is not, according to Fletcher, so much an indication that allegory-telling demands conflict as it is a reflection of the nature of human desire, where conflict and ambivalence almost always do exist. Part way through the novel Slothrop is overcome by his natural sloth-fulness and swings toward destruction rather than salvation as he gives up his quest in order to pursue the mindless pleasures of existence. Most allegorical heroes succeed in their tasks because they are exemplifications of what man might do to save himself. These characters often bear names that suggest their exemplary natures, or they find aid in outside sources in order to overcome what no man could overcome alone. Slothrop is both average and unaided, and so he fails; other characters, such as Enzian, are above average and committed to their tasks, or look for signs from "outside," as the narrator indicates Slothrop should be doing, and may succeed in similar tasks. Generally, however, structures in *Gravity's Rainbow* are not dualistic but pluralistic; it is usually Pointsman and his Pavlovians who are obsessed with "ideas of the opposite" (*GR* 48).

AMBIVALENCE AND AMBIGUITY IN *GRAVITY'S RAINBOW*

The allegorical qualities of *Gravity's Rainbow* which lead some critics to oversimplify the meaning of the novel are rather limited. "Mythic" writing, such as Kafka's, and religious and psychological rituals, which are very similar to allegory, are, in many respects, more descriptive of the narrative and thematic effects of *Gravity's Rainbow* than is allegory itself. The "conflict" that is being extrapolated symbolically in the novel is not constructed upon any moral formula or set of didactic principles, but upon an examination of the conflicting forces themselves, and therefore no preponderant ethical system clearly emerges. The allegorical "moral dualism" of Pynchon's work can be discerned by pairing Pointsman and Mexico, Blicero and Slothrop (or Enzian), Enzian and Tchitcherine, the "two" rockets (Enzian's and Blicero's, or the Manichean good and evil rockets), or the elect and the preterite. But such Manichean dualism must be forced in many respects. For instance, Tchitcherine and Enzian are white and black, just perhaps preterite and elect, but neither favors any of Pointsman's values from the Mexico-Pointsman diad. The reader has a sense that the dopplegängers that permeate the book must be important to the plot and theme, but most often the precise relationships of the doubles are somewhat blurred. The "dualism" in *Gravity's Rainbow* can be understood more clearly in terms of myth, which generally requires the acceptance of an ambivalent imagery, while in true allegory the moral weight generally falls heavily on one side or the other. As Springer tells Slothrop about the preterite: "Be compassionate. But don't make up fantasies about them. Despise me, exalt them, but remember, we define each other. Elite and preterite, we move through a cosmic design of darkness and light, and in all humility, I am one of the very few who can comprehend it *in toto*" (*GR* 495). The narrator has great sympathy for the preterite because he numbers himself among them: like Slothrop, his cards "point only to a long and scuffling future, to mediocrity" (*GR* 738). But his mistrust of the elect is bound up with his paranoia about the future, about the design which, unlike Springer, he cannot see. His ambivalence is clearer in his relation to the rocket as the center of a new religion. According to Freud in *Totem and Taboo,* a taboo object, which the rocket certainly resembles, always represents, in a religious and a psychological sense, both the most desirable (holy) thing and the most repulsive (damning) thing that the mind can conceive.

Yet even this kind of metaphysics is based on the same philosophical "habit" of antithesis as positivist science. It might be more helpful to follow Nietzsche's advice in *Beyond Good and Evil* and not continue to talk about antitheses where there are only degrees and diverse subtle levels.

The apparently dualistic structures of the novel can be seen as structures of the narrator's mind. Each character can be taken not merely in the allegorical sense of representing a single, isolated concept, but in the psychological sense of representing a single complex of thoughts and emotions in the mind of the narrator. Most psychologies accept the premise that almost all thoughts and images encounter, to some degree, both positive and negative responses in the human psyche. A common complaint against Pynchon's method of characterization is that his creatures lack "psychology," but, seen from this vantage point, the narrator of *Gravity's Rainbow* is a complete psychological portrait of a modern creative personality existing in an environment in which, at times, everything seems bent on apocalypse. Nietzsche called the psyche and Jung called the personality the "social structures" of the impulses and the emotions. In a similar sense, the socioeconomic, cultural, political, and technological systems of this novel are part of its "personality"; they structure the narrator's (and the novel's) impulses and emotions. This perspective on narrative point of view that sees the narrator as the central character in his own story is a far cry from the conception of the "omniscient narrator" popularized by Flaubert.

The reader may see the narrator himself as ambivalent toward some of the characters and toward the rocket itself in particular. He tells us, for instance, that "Weissmann's Tarot is better than Slothrop's" (*GR* 746), yet the tarot is described in terms of both vengeful death, which we might expect, and phallic potency, wisdom, strength, and victory. Weissmann gives up the pleasures of the world in order to win the world, but in fulfilling his destiny he becomes an animal, "running on nothing but ice, or less" (*GR* 486). "Better" here may mean simply "more dramatic or conclusive," since Slothrop's tarot points "only to a long and scuffling future, to mediocrity, . . . to no clear happiness or redeeming cataclysm" (*GR* 738). Because the narrator generally seems to affirm life while Blicero seems to affirm death, the reader may wonder at the narrator's enthusiasm for Blicero's tarot. Yet the narrator himself rarely condemns either Blicero or the rocket explicitly, as he does, for instance, Pointsman, whom he frequently portrays as a grasping fool. Actually, however, both Blicero and Pointsman are projections of isolated aspects of the narrator himself, and while the narrator ridicules Pointsman's lust for controlling other individuals, his "will to power," he is also making fun of his own desire to manipulate the characters whom he has created. While describing the Kenosha Colonel's haircut, the narrator splits himself into two distinct personalities, Skippy, who has a childlike passion for digression and "skipping around," and Mr. Information, who is continually dragging Skippy back to the point at hand:

Skippy, you little fool, you are off on another of your senseless and retrograde journeys. Come back, here, to the points. Here is where the paths divided. See the man back there. He is wearing a white hood. His shoes are brown. He has a nice smile, but nobody sees it. Nobody sees it because his face is always in the dark. But he is a nice man. He is the pointsman. He is called that because he throws the lever that changes the points. And we go to Happyville, instead of to Pain City. [*GR* 644]

The narrator's ambivalent attitude toward such things as death, structure, and mindless pleasures manifests itself in conflicting sets of characters and philosophies, each representing one part of the narrator's attitude. When the narrator discusses death from Weissmann's point of view, he totally shares Weissmann's perspective on death as harboring the destiny of man, perhaps his future life. After all, Weissmann is a projected part of the narrator's total vision. What remains ambivalent in these sections is the ultimate meaning of death itself, whether it will bring transformation or merely an end of life. Weissmann is introduced as one who is blindly fulfilling his destiny. In his own paraphrase of Rilke, he is "climbing all alone, terminally alone, up and up into the mountains of primal Pain, with the wildly alien constellations overhead. . . . *And not once does his step ring from the soundless Destiny*" (*GR* 98). This acceptance of death is not apparent in most of the Slothrop sections of the novel, because, at least until the very end of the novel, Slothrop is greatly afraid of dying, as is another part of the narrator. The difference is made apparent in Gottfried's implied comparison to Slothrop as he is put into the 00000:

"The soft smell of Imipolex, wrapping him absolutely, is a smell he knows. It doesn't frighten him. It was in the room when he fell asleep so long ago, so deep in sweet paralyzed childhood . . . it was there as he began to dream. Now it's time to wake, into the breath of what was always real. Come, wake. All is well." [*GR* 754]

Conversely, fear of death and the resulting paranoia can cause great damage. Richard M. Zhluub's desire to wipe out all the hippie nonconformists on the Santa Monica Freeway is somehow, though not "causally," connected to his obsessive fear of death-by-smothering in a plastic bag, recalling the Imipolex shroud of the immediately preceding section of the novel (*GR* 756).

The narrator-as-character shares many of the attributes of his characters, but, unlike the characters, the narrator is always self-conscious about his attitudes, fears, and doubts. Although his paranoia exists, it is controlled and channeled "creatively" into extrapolating both the They-system and the We-system of *Gravity's Rainbow*. The narrator supplies "proverbs for paranoids" ("You may never get in touch with the Master, but you can tickle his creatures" [*GR* 237]), a vision of "the City Paranoic" (*GR* 173), discussions of "operational paranoia" (*GR* 25), Puritanism as paranoia (*GR* 187-89), "anti-paranoia" (*GR* 434), "creative paranoia" (*GR* 638), paranoia induced by drugs, diseases, religions, histories, and situations. His history of Lyle Bland and the Masons is clearly his own creatively paranoid trip:

We would also have to show some interlock between Bland and the Ufa movie-distribution people who sent Pökler out with his advertising bills to Reinickendorf that night, to his fateful meeting with Kurt Mondaugen and the Verein für Raumschiffahrt—not to mention *separate* connections for Achtfaden, Närrisch, and the other S-Gerät people—before we'd have a paranoid structure worthy of the name. Alas, the state of the art by 1945 was nowhere near adequate to that kind of data retrieval. Even if it had been, Bland, or his successors and assigns, could've bought programmers by the truckload to come in and make sure all the information fed out was harmless. Those like Slothrop, with the greatest interest in discovering the truth, were thrown back on dreams, psychic flashes, omens, cryptographies, drug-epistemologies, all dancing on a ground of terror, contradiction, absurdity. [*GR* 582]

Unlike Altieri's modern narrator, Pynchon's narrator participates fully in events, is subject to many of the same ironies as his characters—and is completely aware of these ironies. In the end, the "meaning" of *Gravity's Rainbow* is not to be deciphered so much by filtering out what the narrator says from what the characters say, since the characters are facets of the narrator. What the novel means can only be comprehended

by accepting the narrative point of view as embracing all of the paradoxes and ambiguities that occur. Yet the reader must still carefully weigh
each of the paradoxes and ambiguities. Pynchon's narrative technique
employs devices from expressionist film, the romance novel, allegory and
myth, but, by remaining conscious of the limitations of each of these
narrative forms, he is able to communicate a more complex and multifaceted vision of reality than any of these forms could convey alone.

3

CHARACTERIZATION AND PERSONAL SALVATION

Pynchon's method of characterization—the qualities he examines in his characters and the methods by which he examines them—clarifies a good deal about his treatment of the possibilities for personal salvation in *Gravity's Rainbow*. Unfortunately, both his method of characterization and his attitude toward personal salvation have often been misunderstood.

Clive Jordan was probably speaking for a considerable number of novel readers who are uncomfortable with Pynchon's work when he declared that *Gravity's Rainbow* was flawed because it displayed a lack of human sympathy for its characters. Jordan added that Pynchon's comedy was weakened because the reader could not really "believe" in these characters at all.[1] Jordan's terminology was unfortunately vague, and this vagueness is characteristic of the negative criticism Pynchon has received on this particular aspect of his art. Such critics as Jordan *feel* that the characters are unreal, know that they are somehow different from characters in conventional novels, and yet cannot seem to express either point in a specific and meaningful way. Nor did Jordan, for instance, examine the purposes that might be inherent in distancing the reader from the characters, such as to focus the reader's attention on judging rather than sympathizing with them. In his response to early reviews of *V.* and *The Crying of Lot 49,* James Dean Young has provided an adequate defense of Pynchon's characterization against impressionist criticisms such as Jordan's: "Any argument as to whether or not his characters are 'real' begs the question, for it is simply another way of stating whether or not the reader finds them realistic—like people in real life—or finds them sympathetic."[2] Different readers bring different expectations to a novel, and are willing and able to make different adjustments to the unexpected.

Such a necessarily subjective approach to character analysis is commonly accepted in literary scholarship. For instance, E. M. Forster maintained that a character is real when the novelist can "give us the feeling that, though the character has not been explained, it is explicable."[3] The key phrase "give us the feeling" clearly indicates the relatively subjective nature of this analysis. However, even structuralist criticism, which prides itself on its objectivity, necessarily makes value judgments in matters of interpretation of the relationship of a character to plot and theme. In his widely read early essay on Pynchon, "Pynchon's Tapestries on the Western Wall," Roger Henkle tried to be precise and objective; he maintained that Pynchon has tried unsuccessfully to attain, at crucial moments in *V.* and *The Crying of Lot 49*, "a social realism and full realization through character of philosophical themes."[4] Particularly, Henkle wants Stencil's destiny connected to the corruption of western civilization by more than Stencil's personal whim, since this connection is responsible to a large extent for the relationship between the novel's plot and several of its themes. But Stencil's self-appointed "destiny" is a construction consciously designed by Stencil himself to organize an apparently chaotic reality. He soon loses any distance and objectivity in relation to his fabricated raison d'être, if he ever had any distance; after all, he is despondent without his destiny, and his belief in its reality becomes a matter of psychological survival for him. Sometimes Henkle does not see the irony that Pynchon almost always interjects between a metaphor and the reality it describes, nor does he seem to consider that Pynchon means us to be aware of the arbitrary nature of all such self-appointed "destinies." Otherwise, his response to Stencil would have been different, since the man is then seen as an essentially different character. However, because character analysis is, at least in part, inevitably subjective, Henkle could fairly respond that the reader here is being asked to do too much of the characterizing that Pynchon himself should have done. In an essay delivered at the 1975 MLA convention seminar on Pynchon, Henkle found similar fault with *Gravity's Rainbow*. According to him, the characters are "inadequate to their fictional missions" because they are not fully realized, and they "are not shown in the full complexity and ambiguity of the human social condition."[5]

There seem to be two basic critical objections to Pynchon's method of characterization: first, that Pynchon's characters are not believable because he does not provide the elaborate psychological biographies upon which fiction since Jane Austen has depended so heavily for realistic motivation; second, that Pynchon does not establish convincing connections between a character-as-person and the character's allegorical or symbolic importance. This second point is exemplified by his giving his characters unusual and overtly suggestive or symbolic names, like Miklos Thanatz and Richard M. Zhluub, which sometimes overwhelm what we have come to call the more "realistic" attributes that traditionally suggest the relationship of a character to the work in which he appears. The most sensible way to evaluate these criticisms is to examine what Pynchon has done with characterization in *Gravity's Rainbow*. Then, by exploring the narrator's relationship to the characters, we can approach a clearer understanding of the significance of Pynchon's method of characterization.

Although Pynchon devotes a good deal more time and space to Slothrop than to other figures in the novel, his method of characterizing Slothrop is quite representative of his method of characterization throughout his work and affords the best opportunity for close examination of that method. Slothrop is first introduced to the reader through Teddy Bloat's observation of the materials piled on Slothrop's desk at ACHTUNG (*GR* 18). The reader learns that Slothrop is sloppy, is from Massachusetts, and is interested in popular music, women, puzzles, and current events—on the *News of the World* level. The layers of debris which are described suggest an archeological dig, and in fact Slothrop, at least as suggested by his desk, is a repository of cultural minutiae of the period.

However, as noted in the previous chapter, this catalog of effects is not employed, as it would be in a naturalistic or a realistic fiction, to explain causally Slothrop's behavior. Pynchon's techniques for characterizing Slothrop parody many of the accepted methods of characterization from naturalism and realism. Pynchon both "shows" and "tells" the reader Slothrop's qualities, but he generally stresses the fact, observed by Wayne Booth in *The Rhetoric of Fiction*, that there is often little difference between the two modes of revelation. Typically, Pynchon "shows" and "tells" at the same time, violating even the pretense of narrative objectivity which "showing" presumably indicates.

Because the narrator pervades the consciousnesses of his characters and because he constantly reminds us that he is creating them, we will not be able to respond to them as human beings quite as easily as we might to characters in a work where the pretense of reality is greater. The minds of Pynchon's characters are not directly accessible to the reader through any technique, as is the mind of Stephen Dedalus, for instance, but are always perceived through the narrator. Pynchon emphasizes this fact by overlapping impressionist and expressionist narrative techniques, as has already been shown, as well as by parodying interior monologue (*GR* 145) and stream-of-consciousness narrative techniques, as in the section that records Slothrop's ramblings under sodium amytal. In these parodies Pynchon demonstrates his suspicion of all the narrative techniques of fiction and his sense of their pretentiousness. Pointsman's administration of the "truth serum" hypothetically should reveal the dark secrets locked in Slothrop's subconscious—just as stream-of-consciousness narrative techniques supposedly reveal the real motivations of characters by laying bare their thought processes. However, instead of discovering a precise connection between Slothrop's infant conditioning and the V-2 rocket, Pointsman and the reader are exposed to a much more complex and ambiguous interrelationship between Slothrop's fear of the rocket and his fear of Negroes and excrement, two other things that he associates with blackness. Slothrop's trip down the toilet does display logical connections between the narrator's vision of history and his interpretation of contemporary events. The connections between the character's reality and the thematic concerns of the novel are partly metaphorical, but the human subconscious operates by an associational reasoning process that closely parallels metaphor. The real difficulty here with Pynchon's method of characterization is that the reader who has not accepted the narrator as the main character of the fiction will find this episode even more confusing than it might be, because many of the associations suggested in the dream, especially the historical ones, are not within the scope of Slothrop's consciousness or subconsciousness. Slothrop is not a puppet that the narrator picks up from time to time; he is an integral though limited part of the narrator's personality. Thus, Slothrop knows, even subconsciously, many of the things that the narrator knows, though he does not, of course, have the same breadth of knowledge that the narrator has. The narrator seems to be consciously responsible for most of the obvious irony in Slothrop's thoughts and actions, particularly when the irony has to do with a historical perspective that Slothrop cannot have, as in Slothrop's remarks concerning Malcolm X and John F. Kennedy. Also, the narrator is obviously responsible for structural ironies, such as that of Slothrop's sodium amytal fantasy foreshadowing much of the plot development which follows it.

The concept of the narrator's "creative paranoia," his self-conscious construction of tentative fictional patterns, is necessary for understanding what is being said, particularly in the more fantastic and parodic sections of the novel. The connection between Slothrop's reaction to the rocket and his fantasy involves the fears and desires expressed in his typically American fantasies. These fantasies also belong to the narrator, who is himself attempting to understand their importance. In this sodium amytal dream Slothrop loses his harmonica, his "silver chances of song" (GR 63), and must face his fear of being sodomized by black penises (perhaps his fear of being used for the sport of some great and dark power) and his fear of excrement (perhaps death itself) in order to rescue the harp. Slothrop's harp, like Orpheus's, and like Rilke's poetry and Pynchon's prose, is his means of establishing harmony with life. Slothrop recovers it only when he has achieved peace within himself concerning his fear of death and darkness (*GR* 622). His loss of the harp in the Roseland Ballroom also suggests the loss of the ability of white and black people to harmonize with each other. Narrowly escaping the revenge of Malcolm X, Slothrop muses about the loss of his harmonica (and this harmony): "Might Jack [Kennedy] have kept it from falling, violated gravity somehow?" (*GR* 65). Slothrop's journey down the toilet is a foreshadowing of his odyssey across Europe to discover the new harmony of his age:

Here, in this passage to the Atlantic, odors of salt, weed, decay washing to him faintly like the sound of breakers, yes it seems Jack might have. For the sake of tunes to be played, millions of possible blues lines, notes to be bent from the official frequencies, bends Slothrop hasn't really the breath to do . . . not yet but someday . . . well at least if (when . . .) he finds the instrument it'll be well soaked in, a lot easier to play. A hopeful thought to carry with you down the toilet. [*GR* 65–66]

Slothrop's fantasy is in part too hopeful, and its success is not fully realized in his later quest for the 00000. The fear that propels him after the harp (and after the rocket) also prevents him from breaking out of his isolation when he finds himself in the toilet's inhabited wasteland: "He stands outside all the communal rooms and spaces, outside in his own high-desert morning. [. . .] It's cold. The wind blows. He can feel only his isolation. They want him inside there but he can't join them. Something prevents him: once inside, it would be like taking some kind of blood oath. They would never release him" (*GR* 67).

Pynchon's apparent allusion to Conrad Aiken's narrative poem *The Kid* (here, and to the Kenosha Kid at *GR* 60, 114, 643, 696) identifies Slothrop's fears of his brethren with the American passion for complete independence. The return to freedom and to unity with nature has always been a particularly American theme, and in this respect Slothrop is a typical American protagonist on a quest. *The Kid* describes the westward movement of one of the very first New England settlers, William Blackstone. Aiken extends the westwarding theme to include later Americans from Johnny Appleseed to Daniel Boone and Henry David Thoreau by recording the continued journey of Blackstone's spirit after his death. Aiken says that Blackstone was "the true prototypical American," the ancestor of pioneers who sought freedom and privacy in the open expanse of the West and the physical conquest of an untamed continent, as well as the forerunner of those who struggled for privacy "in the darker kingdoms of the soul." Besides Boone, Appleseed, and Thoreau, Aiken cites Melville and Henry Adams as Blackstone's descendants, "and the outlaws, the lone wolves, the lost souls—yes, these as well."[6] Slothrop's yearnings are as American as his Mom Nadine's apple pie; his failures, such as his failure to accept the community of others because of his instincts for individual freedom, are also particularly American in both Pynchon's and Aiken's versions of the westwarding motif. The Slothrop family business, which converts the green timberland of the Berkshires into "toilet paper, banknote stock, newsprint—a medium or ground for shit, money, and the Word"—entraps the Slothrops: "The three American truths, powering the American mobility, claimed the Slothrops, clasped them for good to the country's fate" (*GR* 28).

Slothrop recovers his harp only after he has accepted the communalism of life in the Zone and his brotherhood with the other Displaced Persons there. In his fantasy it is the approach of another American mythological figure, "Crutchfield or Crouchfield, the westwardman," to the "rhythm of some traditional American tune," that prevents any rapprochement between Slothrop and the inhabitants of this dreamland. When writing of Crutchfield, the narrator speaks with the westwardman's obsessional racism, which in turn is part of Slothrop's subconscious heritage. This "White Cocksman of the *terre mauvais*" is occupied essentially with the sexual subjugation of "both sexes and all animals" (*GR* 69).

Slothrop's fantasies end with, first, the false hope for a harmonious existence patterned by Them (a "Disneyfied" conception of the dead being raised), and then the dashing of that hope on the reality of Roxbury. The political and socio-historical aspects of this fantasy are undeniable, but, rather than receiving a clarification of Slothrop's actual relationship to historical reality, the reader experiences a deepened sense of the emotional confusion that dominates Slothrop's subconscious; as Pynchon suggests of the opening dream of *Gravity's Rainbow*, "This is not a disentanglement from, but a progressive *knotting into*" (*GR* 3). I do not believe that this section supports Josephine Hendin's and like critics' assertions that Slothrop's erections prove that he is in love with his own death. Negroes, particularly the Hereros, are not death to him, but like the rocket are fearsome in some respects, mysterious in others, and suggest a phallic potency which may be either creative or destructive. Slothrop's characterization is necessarily complex, since in many ways he represents the prototypical American and embodies his contradictions and ambiguities.

Pynchon provides information about his characters in a number of ways, making clear that none of these ways is reliable as more than an assertion of the narrator, who is equally responsible for both the interpretation of empirical data and any general observations about the characters. Pynchon employs a variety of metaphorical and naturalistic devices of apparently equal importance. In a typical narrative action, Slothrop himself makes his first appearance to examine a bomb site (*GR* 20). He is shrewd enough to discover that there is some mystery attached to this particular rocket, but is powerless to find out much more. This shrewd-but-not-quite-shrewd-enough pattern describes Slothrop's questing throughout the novel. It is presented through naturalistic detail in this section, but at other times is directly noted by the narrator, who castigates Slothrop for his fateful margin of laziness and insensitivity in tracking down the rocket clues, as during the raid of Peenemünde: "So here passes for him one more negligence . . . and likewise groweth his Preterition sure.... There is no good reason to hope for any turn, any surprise *I-see-it*, not from Slothrop" (*GR* 509). Slothrop's preterition, as it is reflected in the narrative action, seems necessarily to be a matter of free will rather than heavenly inspired election, because the action involves choice. The certainty of Slothrop's preterition "grows" because he fails to act in key moments. Despite the Calvinist paradox that all is foreordained and yet that man has the free will to choose his actions, the reader can only view Slothrop's failure to discover the significance of the 00000 as the result of his pursuit of "the mindless pleasures" of the Zone rather than the true pursuit of his personal grail. Naturalistic novels deal with this deterministic paradox by showing that, whatever the characters do, the parameters of their effectiveness are predetermined by material conditions.

In *Gravity's Rainbow*, however, neither the causes nor the extent of action are clear. The existence of the characters does not necessarily precede their essence, because the search for rocket clues seems to account for their fictional raisons d'étre; however, the reader and the characters are forced into responding as if they were involved in a basically existential situation because forces and goals are unclear. This philosophical paradox is the reason for the apparent contradiction of the narrator's occasional moralizing about Slothrop's betrayal of his quest and his apparent willingness, at the same time, to accept the perverse behavior of Blicero, Thanatz, and others without condemnation. Furthermore, as Richard Hauck has pointed out, the absurdist view in general is relativistic, depending partly if not wholly on the assumption that any value can be judged arbitrary when seen from a point outside the framework which produced the value in the first place. However, this is not a view which discredits the power of moral frameworks.[7] An absurd novel is *about* responding to absurdity, and it defines the protagonist's relationship to it. Literature of the absurd is generally impressionistic; there is little room for a moralizing narrator in a morally relativistic unverise. However, *Gravity's Rainbow* is closer in some ways to the *engagé* novels of existentialism. Creative Paranoia, as a self-consciously fictional construction, parallels to an extent the existentialist's "leap into faith." The narrator himself is a character with one basic assumption to which everything in the novel relates: something has gone wrong in the crucial years of the century, and the apparently catastrophic consequences are still to be fully realized. One of the keys to understanding this novel is in understanding how Slothrop fails, how the plan for his own and his "time's assembly" goes wrong. As an allegorical character, Slothrop is, of course, a man, a type of man, and an exaggeration of a part of all men.

At the novel's start Slothrop's vision has already darkened. He has stopped praying to God (*GR* 24) and is suffering from a "situational paranoia." While a paranoid is generally defined as an individual who is suffering from systematized delusions and projecting hostile forces because he fears imminent destruction, R. D. Laing and others have pointed out that what are considered "delusions" are merely beliefs that differ from the societal norm and that the norm is merely a relative vision that is generally accepted. Obviously, what is generally considered to be true may be false, and what is labeled "delusion" may be a clear vision of reality. Slothrop's fear that every rocket They fire has "his name written on it" (*GR* 25) is not merely an "operational paranoia," a useful supposition consciously adopted, but something that he believes to be true because his experience in wartime London has constantly placed him in contact with death-by-rocket. Slothrop's behavior can justifiably be called paranoid, but Tantivy, the proponent of the "sane" approach, is an early victim of Their conspiracy. In such a situation what is normally called paranoia may become the norm—that is, the normative standard of behavior—and those who do not fear imminent destruction and the hostile system embraced by the concept of They are anti-paranoid, or imperceptive.

Another factor in Slothrop's psycho-biography is important here: "There is in his history . . . a peculiar sensitivity to what is revealed in the sky" (*GR* 20). The religious vision on Constant Slothrop's tombstone depicting the hand of God descending from a cloud (*GR* 26), occurs to Slothrop during the blitz as an apocalyptic comparison to the rocket descending from the sky (*GR* 29), and occurs again in the Zone as a transcendent comparison: "After a heavy rain he doesn't recall, Slothrop sees a very thick rainbow here, a stout rainbow cock driven out of pubic clouds into Earth, green wet valleyed Earth, and his chest fills and he stands crying, not a thing in his head, just feeling natural" (*GR* 626). The relationship of these images to each other will be clarified later in this chapter in the discussion of archetypes. For now it is sufficient to note that, as Slothrop's paranoia dissolves into anti-paranoia (the condition in which *nothing* is connected to anything), he sheds his Puritan heritage along with his penchant for looking for signs. The failure of Slothrop's quest is connected to his failure to observe and interpret signs associated with the rocket technology and with Their conspiracy. However, it is through the shedding of his heritage and of his obsessive interpretation of phenomena that Slothrop gains the measure of peace and joy just described. An understanding of the changes which occur in Slothrop's personality is instrumental in understanding the novel, but the reader must be ready to accept the paradoxes inherent in evaluating characters from several relative points of view.

Often novel readers can evaluate the position of the narrator vis-à-vis the author and thus achieve a degree of certainty about a novel's reality. For instance, in *The Plague* Camus presents a narrator whose words can be judged against the worth of his actions shown in the novel, while in *The Fall* he indicates the narrator's inadequacy in the same way. In *Gravity's Rainbow,* however, there can be no juxtaposition of the evidence of "showing" and of "telling" because the narrator is in such conscious control of both. For example, when recreating what may be the birth of Christ, the narrator asks the reader, "Is the baby smiling, or is it just gas? Which do you want it to be?" (*GR* 131). This self-consciousness is meant to keep the reader at a distance from the characters and the narrative action so that he can observe and judge them more judiciously. At the same time, this technique elevates the information provided through a variety of metaphorical and symbolic devices to the same level as that provided by dramatic showing and narrative telling; rather than simplifying the reader's task of judging the character, this technique compounds it by adding a number of equal, but relative, points of view.

For instance, the quality of shrewd-but-not-quite-shrewd-enough that was noted on the descriptive level at Slothrop's first appearance and by the narrator in the Peenemünde section, is also described on the level of metaphor. Analogy is itself a method of characterization here. Slothrop is described through analogies with religion (the preterite-elect dichotomy of Calvinism), with science ("Personal density . . . is directly proportional to temporal bandwidth"), with high culture (Tannhäuser is a recurrent comparison), with low culture (Rocketman and the comic-book Tyrone of the Floundering Four), with historical figures (Dillinger), and also through the tarot, the *I-Ching,* and astrology. However, the values of these metaphoric revelations are often unclear because each character is a projection of one of the narrator's individual complexes, and therefore the narrator occupies a relatively different position as he describes each character. Because of the source of this imagery, the images may reflect the characters' own obsessions and paranoias, and thus a partial and imbalanced rather than a generally accurate and balanced opinion of the narrator.

A good example of the use of analogy in characterization is the comparison of Slothrop to Tannhäuser, which occurs a half dozen times in the novel. The first reference to Wagner's character seems to be applied by the narrator to the reader as well as to Slothrop:

There is that not-so-rare personality disorder known as Tannhäuserism. Some of us love to be taken under mountains, and not always with horny expectations—Venus, Frau Holda, her sexual delights—no, many come, actually, for the gnomes, the critters smaller than you, for the sepulchral way time stretches along your hooded strolls down here, quietly through courtyards that go for miles, with no anxiety about getting lost . . . no one stares, no one is waiting to judge you . . . out of the public eye . . . even a Minnesinger needs to be alone . . . long cloudy-day indoor walks . . . the comfort of a closed place, where everyone is in complete agreement about Death. [GR 299]

The second important reference to the operatic character, who lost God's grace because he lost himself in the "mindless pleasures" of sensual experience but was redeemed by the miracle of the Pope's blooming staff, is made by Slothrop himself in a fit of delirium:

Later in Berlin, down in the cellar among fever-dreams, [. . .] Slothrop's dumb idling heart sez: The Schwarzgerät is no Grail, Ace, that's not what the G in Imipolex G stands for. And you are no knightly hero. The best you can compare with is Tannhäuser, the Singing Nincompoop—you've been under one mountain at Nordhausen, been known to sing a song or two with uke accompaniment, and don'tcha feel you're in a sucking marshland of sin out here, Slothrop? maybe not the same thing William Slothrop [. . .] meant when he said "sin." . . . But what you've done is put yourself on somebody else's voyage—some Frau Holda, some Venus in some mountain—playing her, its, game . . . you know that in some irreducible way it's an evil game. You play because you have nothing better to do, but that doesn't make it right. And where is the Pope whose staff's gonna bloom for you? [GR 364]

A much more striking reference, because it is an assertion of a cause-and-effect relationship by the narrator, is a line that follows Slothrop's intercourse with Bianca. While making love, Slothrop has imagined himself to be inside of his own penis, which in turn is conceived as being on a rocket flight not unlike Gottfried's in the 00000. At the "detonation" of his orgasm Slothrop hears the "kingly voice of the Aggregat" "announcing the void." It is difficult to accept Slothrop's relationship with Bianca seriously because of her age, but the narrator suggests that this is Slothrop's most poignant and meaningful affair, perhaps the only time he is really moved emotionally during sex:

They have been holding each other. She's been talking about hiding out. [. . .]

He knows she can. He knows. Right here, right now, under the make-up and the fancy underwear, she *exists*, love, invisibility. . . . For Slothrop this is some discovery.

But her arms around his neck are shifting now, apprehensive. For good reason. Sure he'll stay for a while, but eventually he'll go, and for this he is to be counted, after all, among the Zone's lost. The Pope's staff is always going to remain barren, like Slothrop's own unflowering cock. [*GR* 470]

Bianca is emotionally, and perhaps physically, destroyed by Slothrop's departure, by his willingness to lose her ("an American requirement" [*GR* 472]), by his willingness to accept the easy alternative in place of the hard-to-get real thing. The narrator tells us directly in his Tannhäuser analogy that Slothrop will not be saved, even by the Counterforce, because of his inability to accept the responsibility of continually striving to capture the real in the face of great difficulty and little reward. In fact, Slothrop's desertion may actually have triggered Bianca's suicide—it is never clear who, if anyone, murders her—and it is his discovery of her death that causes Slothrop's complete abandonment of his quest.

The song of Tannhäuser that occurs almost two hundred pages later seems to support this analysis:

> Where is the Pope whose staff will bloom for me?
> Her mountain vamps me back, with silks and scents,
> Her oiled, athletic slaves, her languid hints
> Of tortures transubstantiate to sky,
> To purity of light—of bonds that sing,
> And whips that trail their spectra as they fall.
> At weather's mercy now, I find her call
> At every turn, at night's foregathering.
>
> I've left no sick Lisaura's fate behind.
> I made my last confession as I knelt,
> Agnostic, in the radiance of his jewel . . .
> Here, underneath my last and splintering wind,
> No song, no lust, no memory, no guilt:
> No pentacles, no cups, no holy fool. . . . [*GR* 532-33]

The first stanza of the song seems to refer to nature "unredeemed" by any spiritual value—Slothrop's unfortunate, preterite condition; "Gravity's Rainbow" here is the "bonds that sing,/And whips that trail their spectra as they fall." The repetition of the theme of the Pope's staff and the mention of the Fool, which is Slothrop's tarot card, determine that the song is Slothrop's own and that he has accepted Tannhäuser as his emblem, with certain reservations expressed in the second stanza. The ambiguous first line of this stanza could be interpreted to mean that Slothrop has not left behind anyone whose fate depends on him, that he can no longer help either Greta Erdmann, whom the narrator compares to his Lisaura in an earlier section (*GR* 364), or her daughter Bianca, who is already dead; or that Katje, who appears directly after the song, cannot use his help. Since this song occurs shortly after Slothrop's failure to recognize the "holy center" of the rocket at Peenemünde, the radiance of the Pope's jewel before which Slothrop knelt in confession is possibly the rocket itself. However, Slothrop fails to pray at this opportunity (*GR* 510); rather, Bianca's death in the hold of the *Anubis*, which occurs only a few paragraphs before this song, brings him to his knees. Seemingly only before this kind of pain can Slothrop confess. In the last third of the novel, following this epiphany, Slothrop's concerns are almost completely "mindless" and personal; his quest is virtually abandoned.

The last three lines of the song reflect Slothrop's ego dissolution, his loss of will and personal identity, which has begun in earnest by this time. The denial of his tarot identity in the final line indicates that Slothrop has escaped the fate of that identity, but the "escape" is twofold. The Fool is the only card in the tarot deck without a number: that is, he has no set place, but may either begin or end the card cycle. The tarot Fool is a vagabond who exists on the fringe of society, avoiding the containment of rules and taboos. He is ostracized by society, yet is the catalyst that may transform it. He is the harbinger of a new cycle of existence, or renewed life and fresh beginnings. However, in his negative aspect, the Fool pursues extravagant amusements and the joy of the moment, without regard to the chaos he creates. Generally, the Fool indicates an unexpected and unplanned but powerful influence, but if flanked by unfortunate cards, as Slothrop's tarot indicates, he warns of impending error.[8]

Also, in Wagner's opera *Parsifal* the hero is the "holy fool" or "pure fool" ("Fal-Parsi"), rather than merely the traditional grail knight. For Wagner, the grail was not a symbol of chastity, as it is in most versions of the legend, but of charity, of striving, and of human love.[9] (Pynchon's particular references to Tannhäuser, "the singing nincompoop," indicate that he is thinking of Wagner's character rather than of the general folk hero, and his scattered references to the *Ring* cycle make it clear that Pynchon is familiar with Wagner.) The last verse of this song, then, suggests that in order to absolve himself of the mental anguish and paranoia caused by his quest, Slothrop has abandoned the mindful aspects of lust, memory, and guilt—all of which are tied to the ego he loses—as well as his hope for magical transcendence (pentacles), the grail (cups), and his hopes for restoring order and fertility to the kingdom (the task of the holy fool). The mindless pleasures of a non-ego seem all that are left to Slothrop as he scuffles and schleps across the Zone, splintered by the wind so that he occasionally seems to be in several places at once.

This song appears to be a fairly accurate description of Slothrop's fate. Further comparisons of Slothrop with Tannhäuser are made by the narrator, both explicitly, as when Pirate Prentice is sent by the Counterforce to find Slothrop and offer him a special dispensation (*GR* 619), and implicitly, as when Slothrop's indecisiveness, his inability "to come down on one side or another," is translated into the Puritan terminology of "the glozing neuters of the world" (*GR* 677). The peculiar relationship of this kind of analogy to characterization in *Gravity's Rainbow* is apparent in the character's having taken the figure of speech from the narrator and then later passed it back to him. Slothrop approximates Tannhäuser in the mind of the narrator, but this is not a confining, mechanical definition of his character. It is what Slothrop and the narrator—who has a similar tarot—predict or fear for themselves, and particularly what the narrator predicts for Slothrop. "Tannhäuserism" is part symbolism and part psychology, but not completely either. (This combination of affects is somewhat similar to Quentin's construction of Sutpen in *Absalom, Absalom,* except that Quentin is a real paranoid and the narrator of *Gravity's Rainbow* is a creative one.)

Symbolism and psychology merge in consideration of the tarot. As C. G. Jung pointed out in *Psychology and Alchemy,* alchemy, tarot, and the *I-Ching* all contain sophisticated systems for the attainment of psychic integration remarkably similar to Jung's own "process of individuation." It is entirely possible, according to Jung, that these so-called occult practices were actually designed as tools of psychotherapy and consciousness-expansion. The tarot cards and the *I-Ching* hexagrams are, as methods of divination, closer to the Rorschach inkblot test than to a crystal ball. They suggest patterns of experience which the subject fleshes out with his own associations. Like *Gravity's Rainbow* itself, the tarot and *I-Ching* do not predict hard certainties about a static reality, but delineate possibilities for action within the dynamic interrelationships of an individual and society. The Fool is not merely an allegorical role to be filled by a walking obsession, but a personality type with several distinct possibilities for success or failure. According to A. E. Waite, whom Pynchon credits as his tarot authority (*GR* 738), the Fool is initially a fair-haired youth who wears a richly decorated costume of green and gold, not unlike Slothrop's Rocketman outfit. He carries a satchel of indigo leather suspended from an ebony wand, and in the other hand, a white rose. His card shows him skipping happily along, his eyes fixed on a silver butterfly which flutters before his face. He seems unaware of the cliff face looming beneath his feet or of the dog snapping at his leg, perhaps in warning.[10] According to tarot exegetes, the silver butterfly may represent either the distracting sensual pleasures of the natural world or the Spirit of Life leading the Fool on to new adventures and higher attainments, and both of these interpretations seem to be possibilities for Slothrop at various times.

The narrator, who we would assume knows at the beginning of the novel exactly how Slothrop will finally fail, never seems to reconcile himself to that disappointment—perhaps because Slothrop does not exist for him as an icon but as a complex entity with various potentials, or perhaps merely because Slothrop is such a major part of himself. The narrator also identifies himself as "born a joker" and appears in "something green-striped, pantalooned, and ruffled," the tarot Fool's uniform (*GR* 122). While the narrator becomes increasingly sure of Slothrop's failure, he, like Slothrop, does not really give up until well after the battle seems lost, if then. Another tarot card that the narrator shares with Slothrop, the three of pentacles reversed, indicates effort which results in disappointment and failure, just criticism from those one respects, obstinacy, and conceit or prejudice which makes one unable to benefit from the advice or experience of others.[11] The narrator's unwillingness to give himself over completely to pessimism, which some critics have maintained is an optimism that Pynchon intends as a balance for the grimness of inevitable apocalypse, is actually the narrator's rather stormy working-out of the development of Slothrop's psyche and perhaps his own.

Characterization in *Gravity's Rainbow* is not a forced union of symbolic allegory and realistic but discontinuous character traits, but an organic marriage of mythic structures and human psychologies which have been tested against various socio-cultural situations for thousands of years. Traditional characterization assumes that the personality has a single known identity and structure. Pynchon's method of characterization suggests that such an assumption is fallacious, that personality is a complex interaction between the individual and his environment; his characters are likely to identify with and adopt certain characteristics from their socioeconomic roles, although they will not be defined by those roles.

Considering the wealth of information about his characters that Pynchon has supplied, it is difficult to agree with those critics who maintain that Pynchon's characters are flat or sketchy. In *Aspects of the Novel*

E. M. Forster maintains that a character is real if the novelist gives us the feeling that, whether or not the character has been completely explained, he is explicable. However, Forster adds that this is a reality of a kind we don't get in daily life. In our common intercourse we do not understand each other except in a general way, and we cannot reveal ourselves fully even when we want to; "intimacy" and "perfect knowledge" are illusions.[12] The first part of Forster's statement parallels Young's remarks quoted at the beginning of this chapter: a character is "real" when the reader believes that he could have an existence outside of the novel. It seems to me that a number of characters in *Gravity's Rainbow*, especially Roger and Jessica (as in the section about their winter evening in Kent [*GR* 124-36]), and Slothrop, fulfill Forster's criterion for "real" characters as well as some of the best characters in fiction do. Even when Pynchon seems to be emphasizing the ways in which his characters differ from the more conventional products of realism, Slothrop is convincing and moving:

At a farmhouse in a river valley far south of Rostock, he comes in to shelter out of the midday rain, falls asleep in a rocking chair on the porch, and dreams about Tantivy Mucker-Maffick, his friend from long ago. He has come back, after all and against the odds. It's somewhere out in the country, English country, quilted in darkened green and amazingly bright straw-yellow, of very old standing rocks on high places, of early indenture to death and taxes, of country girls who walk out at night to stand naked on the tor and sing. Members of Tantivy's family and friends have come, all in a mood of quiet celebrating, because of Tantivy's return. Everybody understands it's only a visit: that he will be "here" only in a conditional way. At some point it will fall apart, from thinking about it too much. There is a space of lawn cleared for dancing, with a village band and many of the women dressed in white. After a spell of confusion about the day's schedule of events, the meeting takes place—it seems to be underground, not exactly a grave or crypt, nothing sinister, crowded with relatives and friends around Tantivy who looks so *real*, so untouched by time, very clear and full of color . . . "Why, Slothrop."
   "Oh—where've you *been*, gate?"
   "'Here.'"
   "'"Here"'?"
   "Yes, like that, you've got it—once or twice removed like that, but I walked in the same streets as you, read the same news, was narrowed to the same spectrum of colors. . . ."
   "Then didn't you—"
   "I didn't *do* anything. There was a change."
   The colors in here—stone facing, flowers worn by guests, the strange chalices on the tables—carry an underbreath of blood spilled and turned black, of gentle carbonizing in the blank parts of the cities at four o'clock on Sunday afternoon . . . it makes crisper the outlines of Tantivy's suit, rather a gigolo suit of unspeakably foreign cut, certainly nothing he ever would have thought of wearing. . . .

"I guess we don't have much time . . . I know this is shitty, and really selfish but I'm so alone now, and . . . I heard that just after it happens, sometimes, you'll sort of hang around for a while, sort of look after a friend who's 'here.' . . ."

"Sometimes." He is smiling: but his serenity and distance are the stretch of an impotent cry past Slothrop's reach.

"Are you looking after me?"

"No. Slothrop, not you. . . ."

Slothrop sits in the old weathered rocker looking out at a rolling line of hills and the sun just come down out of the last of the rainclouds, turning the wet fields and the haycocks to gold. Who passed by and saw him sleeping, his face white and troubled nodded on the breast of his muddy uniform? [*GR* 551-52]

I, for one, saw him, but then both perception and character believability are to a large extent subjective.

The second part of Forster's statement, concerning the difference between a "real" character and a real person, is certainly appropriate to some of the changes which Pynchon has made in his characterization, and in this sense the presentation of his characters is perhaps more "realistic" than are those of many so-called realists.

A number of critics have realized that Pynchon's method of characterization emphasizes the outside forces which operate on his characters and with which his characters interact, rather than the particularly affective aspects of personality which have been the bases of characterization in most twentieth-century fiction.[13] This emphasis is the result of two concerns central to Pynchon: first, his concern with matters of perception and interpretation primary to any matter of identity; and second, his concern for enormous political, economic, and socio-cultural forces which overwhelm the individual. Like people in the real world, Pynchon's characters are greatly affected by their social roles. For instance, even the violently unfeminine Frau Gnahb is seen by her son Otto as a staunch participant in the same "Mother Conspiracy" (*GR* 505) to which Nadine Slothrop subscribes and which Leni Pökler avoids only by giving up her child and her husband (*GR* 219-20). Enzian becomes totally consumed by his leadership role (*GR* 660), while Slothrop travels in the opposite direction, escaping his role only by divesting himself totally of his ego, his sense of self.

At the same time, Pynchon does provide more or less standard psychological biographies for many characters such as Slothrop, Enzian, and Katje. While problems of perception and interpretation of reality external to the characters are certainly central to the theme and plot of *Gravity's Rainbow*, they are very much related to problems of identity, of which Slothrop's ego dissolution is the most obvious. A narrative point of view that focuses exclusively on the internal manifestations of character, as does that of *Ulysses,* emphasizes the internal activity of the mind but is very much concerned with problems of perceiving and interpreting the external world; Pynchon's point of view may be seen as emphasizing the external world, but in one respect the story exists in the narrator's mind, and is the representation of the narrator-as-character's internal reality, in the manner of *Finnegans Wake.*

The second criticism raised against Pynchon's method of characterization at the beginning of the chapter was that his characters are not always realistically connected to their symbolic or allegorical roles, and that they are, for instance, encumbered with names and actions that are overtly suggestive or symbolic and that sometimes overshadow what we traditionally recognize as the more realistic attributes suggesting the relationship of a character to a novel. However, as Forster indicates, the relationship of character to fiction is never "realistic" in terms of the relationship of a human to environmental reality, but is merely traditionally accepted as real. If Pynchon makes readers uncomfortable in his characterization, I suspect that it is often because he violates their expectations by doing too much rather than because he does too little. The names he gives his characters are no more unbelievable than are those of the Watergate conspirators, as George Levine has pointed out,[14] and no one recognized the plot of *that* conspiracy for quite a while. Also, there is the tradition of Dickens, Smollet, and Thackeray to lend authority to Pynchon's use of unusual names. Slothrop's name may suggest "slothfulness," "rop" perhaps suggesting "run-of-paper" advertisements which do not have any set place. But in fact, William Slothrop himself was a real New England Pilgrim who arrived in the same fleet as Pynchon's own ancestor William in 1630.[15] Nor are the names of other major characters implausible, despite their suggestiveness. Of course, reality itself is often unbelievable and makes for bad art, but minor characters, such as Bloody Chiclitz, often seem designed by Pynchon precisely to outrage the reader's sense of verisimilitude. Because "Chiclitz" and similar names are inessential for the realization of plot and theme, it seems probable that Pynchon does this to reinforce the relationship between a character and his role and to remind the reader that he is engaged in a self-consciously constructed fiction.

Slothrop's dispersal, however, appears to be a much more strictly "unrealistic" device of metaphor for the purposes of characterization, of the kind usually found only in myth and its derivative forms, allegory, fairy tale, and perhaps science fiction, where levels of internal and external reality are not so clearly differentiated. Romance fiction, to which *Gravity's Rainbow* bears certain similarities, generally tries to convince the reader that its supernatural phenomena are somehow actual and externally real. The mythic or symbolic features of these phenomena are often minimal. On the other hand, one need only look to Kafka's *Metamorphosis* for a modern example of a bizarre supernatural event, completely unexplainable on a naturalistic level except as a possible delusion of an unreliable narrator, but which is, nevertheless, powerfully convincing and essentially mythic at the same time. As with the tarot, the mythic in Kafka parallels the psychological; the reader who appreciates Kafka realizes, either consciously or preconsciously, that however unrealistic on the natural level, his stories are "true" on the mythic or psychological level. A myth is "true" if it recapitulates, in some way, the collective psychological and physiological experience of a people. Pynchon, like Kafka, is often more concerned with conveying psychic and mythic truth than with conveying a sense of mimetic reality which we know to be a simplistic, subjective construction in the first place. Slothrop's dispersal is largely a metaphorical state with important implications for the psychological state of the narrator, as well as for himself, and for the mythological reality of western civilization. One may finally maintain that Pynchon's characters are not "realistic" like Henry James's are—but that they are "true" in another way. (It is worth noting that E. M. Forster found James's characters to be limited and bloodless "deformities."[16]) No doubt Pynchon does occasionally sacrifice the reader involvement generated by verisimilitude in order to distance the reader and to stimulate a more objective judgment of the characters' actions. Essentially, however, the reader's response to Pynchon's characters will depend on the expectations, and the flexibility, that the reader brings to the novel.

IMPLICATIONS OF CHARACTERIZATION FOR THEME AND PLOT

So far, I have discussed the manner in which Pynchon creates his characters and why he does so. The true test of these remarks, however, is to show how they lead to a greater understanding of the novel and how these characters exist in relationship to our own psychological reality.

I have suggested that Pynchon creates characters by first creating a narrative persona and then populating the narrator's psychological terrain with characters who are both mythically and psychologically allegorical. Furthermore, I have suggested that every important character in the novel represents a complex of thoughts and feelings that originally belongs to the narrator, and that therefore the narrator shares most of their impulses to some degree. While the same could be said of many novels, this manner of looking at narrative point of view is particularly appropriate for *Gravity's Rainbow*. The psychological responsibility of the narrator for even the least sympathetic characters, such as Pointsman, does not necessitate his conscious agreement with them. As Jung maintained, humans don't hold "either/or" conceptions of reality, but "either and or" conceptions, in a manner similar to modern physicists' simultaneous maintenance of "contradictory hypotheses" of light—as wave and as particle.

For many decades "realistic" characters have been those that fulfilled certain psychological profiles and patterns, many of which were canonized by Freud. Both naturalists and realists manipulated these profiles which, when rigged to fit the mechanics of behaviorism, make possible a positivist cause-and-effect analysis of character. Later psychologists determined that Freud was probably simplistic in his crediting of sexuality as the prime mover of the psyche and in his overemphasis of the importance of infancy as the period when the seeds of nearly all personality disorders are planted. By 1912 Jung was showing that the psyche is motivated, shaped and reshaped, by a variety of "complexes," and remains in dynamic flux throughout its existence.

Jung saw that both our culture and the individuals of our time suffer from a lack of any central unconditional value on which to base decisions of any complexity. On the other hand, Freudian analysis paralleled the disintegrative cultural movement of the last hundred years. Scientists showed that physical reality can be reduced to subatomic particles; artists broke up colors into constituent primary tones, surfaces into constituent planes, and objects into subjectively felt elements; in music conventional harmonic intervals gave way to dissonances, giving rise to jazz (Pynchon notes Yardbird Parker "finding out how he can use the notes at the higher ends of these very chords to break up the melody" [*GR* 63]); in literature surrealist poetry and works like *Finnegans Wake* used disconnected words for their evocative power and associational suggestiveness. Pynchon's encyclopedic narrative is an attempt not only to document the disintegrative tendencies of our time but to reintegrate them in a Jungian fashion.

Freudian psychoanalysis analyzes every psychic manifestation down to its lowest common denominator, reduces every value to a derivative of family drama or infantile sexuality. According to most modern psychologists, the result is mechanistic, materialistic, very pessimistic, and usually unhelpful. Jung, however, identified the individual human psyche as the ultimate unifying value of our time. As Eleanor Bertine has noted, Jung's greatest contribution is that the supreme value sought for centuries by religion and mysticism actually lies within the human psyche itself. Jung elaborated a method by which it can be sought there, without the necessity of any dogma or belief. In addition, this method can be formulated in terms consonant with modern science.[17] Without denying the relativity of personal experience or the Heraclitean flux of the cosmos, Jung was able to provide a constant point of reference and a pattern for psychological reintegration and salvation. Although Pynchon has not patterned his characters on Jungian stereotypes, the specific features of Jung's analytical psychology clarify the narrator's relationship to his characters in a number of ways.

Jung maintains that the "psyche," by which he means the totality of conscious and unconscious psychic processes, is a whole that should be developed to the greatest possible degree of differentiation, coherence, and harmony. Man must constantly guard against the breakup of the psyche into separate, autonomous, and conflicting systems: this type of dissociation marks a deformation of the personality. The function of the psyche known as the ego organizes the conscious mind and controls awareness, protecting the consciousness from being overwhelmed by experience. Ego selection of material that is allowed to penetrate the consciousness maintains a continuous quality of coherence in the individual personality. The ego of a highly "individuated" person, one who is psychically whole and distinctly individual, will allow more things to become conscious than will that of a less healthy personality. For instance, as Slothrop's personality becomes less whole and begins to disintegrate into parts midway through *Gravity's Rainbow,* the narrator applies Mondaugen's Law to him: "Personal density is directly proportional to temporal bandwidth," bandwidth being "the width of your present, your now.... The more you dwell in the past and in the future, the thicker your bandwidth and the more solid your persona" (*GR* 509). Jung noted that ideas and memories that evoke anxiety are apt to be refused admittance to consciousness, espeically in poorly individuated personalities. At the same time, very strong experiences can almost always batter their way into the consciousness. Slothrop's dispersal may, then, be caused by his psychological inability to suffer the painful memories of the experiences that overwhelm him on his quest for the rocket or the equally traumatic thoughts of his future. Essentially, the elements of the narrator's and Slothrop's personalities are not well integrated to begin with, particularly on the unconscious level; Slothrop disintegrates, and the narrator fragments himself into characters. On the other hand, the narrator distrusts the ego because, in adapting the individual for life in the material world, it generally does so on Their terms:

Well, if the Counterforce knew better what those categories concealed, they might be in a better position to disarm, de-penis and dismantle the

Man. But they don't. Actually they do, but they don't admit it. Sad but true. They are as schizoid, as double-minded in the massive presence of money, as any of the rest of us, and that's the hard fact. The Man has a branch office in each of our brains, his corporate emblem is a white albatross, each local rep has a cover known as the Ego, and their mission in this world is Bad Shit. We do know what's going on, and we let it go on. As long as we can see them, stare at them, those massively moneyed, once in a while. As long as they allow us a glimpse, however rarely. We need that. [*GR* 712-13]

According to Jung, man is born a psychological whole, but during the course of his life this wholeness is disturbed and unbalanced as the personality attempts to differentiate itself in response to individual experience. One no longer responds unconsciously from an instinctually unified base of thinking, feeling, intuiting, and sensing, but differentiates these functions so that a conscious decision can be made, for instance, purely from the function of thinking and without regard to feeling. These four functions must first be made conscious, and then a comfortable interrelationship which does not sacrifice one function to another must be developed. A personality may become deformed if it tries to repress basic impulses which, in any event, will either be sublimated or realized through psychotic or neurotic activity. The wholeness of a child or a primitive man differs from that of an adult or that of a member of a complex society in that the primitive is instinctively and unconsciously whole, while the latter, who has differentiated the unconsciousness and the consciousness, has passed beyond this possibility for unity, and must reconcile the opposing elements of the personality through a normally arduous process. Dodson-Truck notes, in *Gravity's Rainbow,* that the Old Norse rune for *S* was originally a graphic representation of the sun: "The Goths, much earlier, had used a circle with a dot in the center. This broken line evidently dates from a time of discontinuities, tribal fragmenting perhaps, alienation—whatever's analogous, in a social sense, to the development of an independent ego by the very young child" (*GR* 206). Recovering psychic unity becomes the ultimate goal of Jungian analysis. In *Gravity's Rainbow* the narrator himself is undergoing this process, and his characters are frequently depicted in pairs because each of them—Pointsman on the one hand, Mexico on the other—reflect differentiated and unreconciled functions, and each represents an opposite response to an experience.

Pynchon does not seem to interpret consciously the Jungian process of individuation or the tarot cycle in *Gravity's Rainbow,* nor is every aspect of these two patterns realized in the novel. However, these patterns illuminate Pynchon's characters and explain some of the peculiarities of the novel. Pynchon is familiar with Jung, and uses his system of archetypes quite openly: "It was nice of Jung to give us the idea of an ancestral pool in which everybody shared the same dream material" (*GR* 410). He also mentions three other psychological theorists whose systems figure in *Gravity's Rainbow*. Wolfgang Köhler was a Gestalt psychologist who postulated that humans visualize the world in terms of patterns; his work contributed significantly to the theory of cybernetics, a theory of communication that could be used to suggest that paranoia is a way of organizing experiential input. The narrator parodies Freud's ideas in the exaggerated Oedipal conflict between Tyrone and his Perilous Pop in the adventures of the Floundering Four, but this idea is treated more seriously in terms of the plot of the novel, where Slothrop's father actually has stolen his "Radiant Hour" by selling his son to the IG, and in the narrator's remark that "fathers are carriers of the virus of Death, and sons are infected" (*GR* 723). Finally, of course, there is Pavlov, who has a loving son in Pointsman.

It is Jungian psychology that seems most directly applicable to the characters of the novel. Jung maintained, amidst great controversy, that the mind of each man is prefigured by evolution; that is, the brain itself has inheritable physical elements that prefigure the conscious and unconscious structures of mentality and thereby predetermine, to an extent, that every person will react to life's experiences within a certain set of parameters. Jung posited that a part of the unconscious mind, the "collective unconscious," is a reservoir of primordial images called archetypes. The archetypes are predispositions or potentialities for experiencing and responding to the world. Because the archetypes (often portrayed in myth) unite the development of the human species with the development of the individual psyche, these archetypes are appropriate for showing how the plot of *Gravity's Rainbow* involves the parallel developments of the narrator's psyche and the socio-cultural condition of modern man. In the novel the rocket is an archetype of phallic potentiality that accrues to itself a complex of other archetypes, such as the tarot Tower and the yew tree. For this reason, the rocket means different things to different people, yet retains a consistency in many of its aspects:

But the Rocket has to be many things, it must answer to a number of different shapes in the dreams of those who touch it—in combat, in tunnel, on paper—it must survive heresies shining, unconfoundable . . . and heretics there will be: Gnostics who have been taken in a rush of wind and fire to chambers of the Rocket-throne . . . Kabbalists who study the Rocket as Torah, letter by letter—rivets, burner cup, and brass rose, its text is theirs to permute and combine into new revelations, always unfolding . . . Manicheans who see two Rockets, good and evil, who speak together in the sacred idiolalia of the Primal Twins (some say their names are Enzian and Blicero) of a good Rocket to take us to the stars, an evil Rocket for the World's suicide, the two perpetually in struggle. [*GR* 727]

There are principal archetypes that shape personality itself because they are very likely to become the seeds around which experiences cling to form complexes. Each individual has a "persona" archetype that enables him to portray a character that is not necessarily his own in order to effect a favorable impression. Psychologically, the healthy individual may have a number of personas that aid him in social and commercial life. This concept of persona is well known in literature and is generally applicable to any narrative voice.

While the persona is the outward face of the psyche that the world sees, the inward face is called the "anima" in males and the "animus" in females; the anima archetype is the female side of the male psyche, and the animus archetype is the male side of the female psyche. Psyches are not actually androgynous, but they contain archetypal characteristics of their opposites that aid the sexes in understanding each other. Weissmann's bisexuality and his tarot, in which he is crossed by the Queen of his suit, both represent aspects of his anima: the Queen is "perhaps himself, in drag. She is the chief obstacle in his way" (*GR* 748). As the Knight of Swords, Weissmann is courageous, strong, and highly skilled, and his presence indicates the approach of battles that must be fought and enemies that must be defeated by strength of arms. The queen is devious and expert at half truth and quiet slander; her keen intellect makes her a dangerous enemy. Weissmann is an agent of fate, a man driven by a destiny that appears inevitable. As such, he may not retain a normal personality; he must exorcise himself of many of the characteristics of his anima that are vain, helpless, and uncertain, and that would lead him astray from his fated path. His voracious bisexuality seems to indicate his passion to dominate in every guise, as They dominate the passive Us throughout most of *Gravity's Rainbow,* but also his passion to submit just as completely, and thereby to perfect his union with the world. As Thanatz suggests, perhaps They have outlawed certain sexual practices because They need all of our capacities for dominance and submission to keep Their chain of command in working order. Thus, the narrator frequently refers to bureaucrats and other keepers of Their laws as "sucking the cock of authority." Weissmann's launching of Gottfried in the 00000 is a ritual attempt at breaking through Their sexual restraints to transcendence. Weissmann's perversity is directed at disrupting the normal patterns of behavior, as are the antics of the Counterforce, and he pays the price of sanity for that breakthrough.

The most powerful of the personality archetypes is the "shadow," which contains much of man's basic animal nature. During socialization the animal spirits contained in the shadow are suppressed by the development of a strong persona. Civilization is gained, however, at the expense of spontaneity, creativity, strong emotions, deep insights, and the wisdom of instinctual nature. In a healthy person the ego and the shadow work in close harmony, but society's natural inclination toward repressing the shadow tends to create an imbalance in this relationship. Jung wrote at the end of World War I that the animal in man only becomes more beastlike when repressed, and advanced this as the reason why Christianity, which categorically represses the animal in man, has been responsible for the bloodiest wars in the history of the world. Tchitcherine, civilization's man of metal, believes that Enzian is his shadow and must therefore be destroyed for the sake of his survival, but he himself is nearly destroyed by this obsession. On the other hand, in giving himself up to his destiny, Weissmann succumbs almost completely to the shadow, becoming more and more animalistic (*GR* 486). He is crossed by his intellect and can only succeed by asserting his instincts.

In Jung's system the central archetype of the personality is the "self," the archetype of order, organization, and unification. The self unites the personality by harmonizing the other archetypes; this state of selfhood and self-realization is the ultimate goal of every personality and is usually achieved only after a long and difficult psychological process. Blicero is moving in the opposite direction from self-realization because he is obsessed with his destiny. Slothrop fails in his destiny and also suffers the disintegration of his personality. First he is split into the multiple personalities of Scuffling, Schlepzig, and Rocketman, and then he loses all sense of his self as he forgets his scattered ego. However, according to Jung, this is a condition from which the true self may be reborn. In *Psychology and Alchemy,* Jung found the process of individuation to parallel the tarot cycle in many respects. The Fool is the unconscious innocent without self-awareness, whose wholeness is shattered by exposure to the forces of the world, male and female, material and spiritual— represented by the cards of the Emperor, who resembles Pointsman, and the High Priestess, who resembles Katje. Next in the process the individual should become a responsible lover and adjust himself to society. Slothrop's failure to develop in these respects has been noted. The process has thus far been lopsided in its development of the conscious mind at the expense of the unconscious, and the individual must reexamine himself under the auspices of the Hermit if he is to develop. The solitary stages of Slothrop's wanderings in the Zone suggest this process. The Hermit must reorient himself by realizing that his apparently insurmountable difficulties are common to all mankind. Only then can he arrive at the stage personified by the only card besides the Fool which we know for certain is in Slothrop's tarot, the Hanged Man. Jung says the Hanged Man represents the renouncing of the past material life in favor of an uncertain future which may bring spiritual fulfillment. But Slothrop's Hanged Man is reversed, suggesting that he cannot make this transition because of his unwillingness to recognize the spiritual signs that fill his world and because of his paranoia. It seems certain in the novel that Slothrop can never achieve reintegration at this level—we are told that his preterition is sealed because of his ignorance of the spiritual and are also informed that he can never be reassembled after he disintegrates; although he does seem to achieve some kind of peace through the loss of ego, neither Slothrop nor "his time" can be properly assembled because they do not recognize important spiritual values.

The next card in the cycle is Death, often called Transformation, recalling the von Braun epigraph in the beginning of *Gravity's Rainbow*. It calls for transcendence of the ego so that the individual may go on to the second half of the cycle. The reversed Hermit, however, fears change. The narrator's pessimism about Slothrop seems to be tied to his fear that death will not lead to transformation; yet, Slothrop does seem to be achieving some kind of preconscious psychic reintegration, late in the story, on

days when in superstition and fright he could *make it all fit,* seeing clearly in each [scrap of refuse] an entry in a record, a history: his own, his winter's, his country's . . . instructing him, dunce and drifter, in ways deeper than he can explain. [. . .] And now, in the Zone, later in the day he became a crossroad, after a heavy rain he doesn't recall, Slothrop sees a very thick rainbow here, a stout rainbow cock driven down out of the pubic clouds into Earth, green wet valleyed Earth, and his chest fills and he stands crying, not a thing in his head, just feeling natural. . . . [*GR* 626]

The crossroad is a variant of the mandala, which itself appears several times in earlier parts of the same passage; the mandala is a Jungian archetype for the unity of all the other archetypes through a Transcendent Function, the union of the different pairs of psychic opposites in a synthesis that transcends them both. It is also Enzian's rocket symbol, and, thanks to a rare bit of extratextual information from Pynchon, we can be fairly certain that Pynchon sees the Hereros as seekers of unity. Joseph Slade cites a letter Pynchon wrote to Thomas F. Hirsch in 1968 saying he could not forget the Hereros' religion, which stresses a unified and integrated tribal life and a pantheistic approach to the universe; this religion had enabled the preliterate, precolonialized, prerationalized Hereros to view the world as a metaphysical whole and to accept paradox as the law of experience. In the Herero view, said Pynchon, opposites can be reconciled and men can be individual selves and yet parts of a larger self, members of a human and a cosmic community.[18] The Herero word for God means both creation and destruction; Slothrop's erections in anticipation of the rocket are not necessarily a suggestion that he is in love with his own death, but, as Jung would say, that his subconscious recognizes the ineluctable interrelationship between life and death.

One conclusion that can be drawn from this examination of Slothrop's final fate is that Slothrop breaks into a variety of personae, none of whom is elect, completely balanced, unified, or able to cope with Their pressures, because he refuses to accept death as a natural aspect of life. He does achieve some sort of emotional or intuitive unification, similar to Buber's I-Thou relationship, by abandoning the ego that caused him to play Their game in the first place, but he does not attain the Jungian wholeness that might have been either a result of his quest or a condition for its successful completion. Therefore, he disappears from society.

If he had wanted to, Pynchon could have used several other facets of Jung's theory in his work. Slothrop's erections, for instance, are only clumsily explained by Pointsman as the "ultra-paradoxical effect" of Slothrop's infant conditioning (GR 90). Jung, together with the physicist Wolfgang Pauli and the biologist Paul Kammerer, developed a theory that could have accounted for Slothrop's behavior; "synchronicity," as it is called, is an explanation for extrasensory phenomena that dovetails nicely with both Pynchon's and Jung's use of the archetype. Synchronicity supplements causality in precisely the manner that Mexico, Leni Pökler, and others suggest some low of correspondences must operate: "Not produce . . . not cause. It all goes together. Parallel, not series. Metaphor. Signs and symptoms. Mapping on to different coordinate systems" (GR 159). Jung defines synchronicity as a coincidence in time of two or more causally unrelated events which have the same or similar meaning, in the form of a coincidence of inner perceptions, such as dreams, visions, or hunches, with the outward events situated in the past, present, or future. Jung goes on to call the archetype "the introspectively recognizable form of a priori psychic orderedness."[19] Thus, it would be only natural for the rocket archetype in Slothrop to seek correspondences in sexual procreativity as well as in the V-2s.

In his early book on Pynchon, Joseph Slade wisely called attention to Kammerer's similar theory of "seriality," a force in some respects comparable to universal gravity. However, unlike gravity, which acts indiscriminately on all mass, seriality acts selectively on form and function to bring similar configurations together in time and space.[20] For Jung, archetypes (of which, in the novel, the rocket definitely seems to be a form) are living psychic forces that make themselves known through a kind of behavioral phenomena that Pynchon attributes to Slothrop.

SLOTHROP'S FATE

Although these observations shed some light on Slothrop's disintegration, his "plucking the albatross of self" (GR 623), a more complete analysis of the metaphoric structures of Gravity's Rainbow is necessary before we can draw any final conclusions about his fate. For instance, Mondaugen's "electro-mysticism" defines the triode as the basic symbol of identity:

Think of the ego, the self that suffers a personal history bound to time, as the grid. The deeper and true self is the flow between cathode and plate. The constant, pure flow. Signals—sense data, feelings, memories relocating—are put onto the grid, and modulate the flow. We live lives that are waveforms constantly changing with time, now positive, now negative. Only at moments of great serenity is it possible to find the pure, the informationless state of signal zero. [GR 404]

Pökler is seen hunting for his true self "across the zero, between the two desires, personal identity and impersonal salvation" (GR 406). Enzian, we are told, is "closest to the zero" among the Germans and Hereros because he has the general serenity that comes from the Herero acceptance of the world. Slothrop seems to achieve this "informationless state," but by pulling free of the grid, by losing his self that suffers a personal history bound to time. Therefore, Enzian can still function in the world and Slothrop cannot.

Slothrop fails to fulfill his destiny but seems to succeed, through the loss of the self that causes man to be egocentrically irresponsible to nature, to find harmony with the world. It does not seem likely that he will regain the self, because he has denied the existence of his outer, conscious life in order to salvage the inner, unconscious life. His failure with Bianca is tied to his loss of temporal bandwidth, his unwillingness or inability to make present concessions for the sake of his future. The passages that describe Slothrop's tranquility near the end of the novel, his unthinking peace with nature and his new vision of the rainbow, are indeed memorable, but it must be observed that Slothrop pays a price. His final "sightings" are painful and poignant: "he has become one plucked albatross. Plucked, hell—stripped. Scattered all over the Zone.

It's doubtful if he can ever be 'found' again, in the conventional sense of 'positively identified and detained.' Only feathers . . ." (*GR* 712). Near the end of the novel, in the Chicago Bar,

> Seaman Bodine looks up suddenly, canny, unshaven face stung by all the smoke and unawareness in the room. He's looking straight at Slothrop (being one of the few who can still see Slothrop as any sort of integral creature any more. Most of the others gave up long ago trying to hold him together, even as a concept—"It's just got too remote" 's what they usually say). Does Bodine now feel his own strength may someday soon not be enough either: that soon, like all the others, he'll *have* to let go? *But somebody's got to hold on, it can't happen to all of us—no, that'd be too much . . . Rocketman, Rocketman. You poor fucker.*
> . . . .
> It wasn't their last meeting, but later on there were always others around, doper-crises, resentments about burns real or intended, and by then, as he'd feared, Bodine was beginning, helpless, in shame, to let Slothrop go. In certain rushes now, when he sees white network being cast in all directions on his field of vision, he understands it as an emblem of pain or death. [*GR* 740–41]

After this passage the only presentation of Slothrop is in "The Occupation of Mingeborough" (*GR* 744), in which there no longer seems to be any hope of Slothrop's return.

It will not do to respond to Slothrop's failure or to the beauty of the small personal success he achieves separately; the interspersing of these sections demands that we see one as a condition of the other. Slothrop escapes his "fate" at Putzi's as well as at Peenemünde; just as for Pökler's daughter Ilse there is both good and bad in that escape. She is last seen "riding lost through the Zone on a long freight train that never seems to come to rest." But: "She will not be used. There is change, and departure: but there is also help when least looked for from the strangers of the day, and hiding, out among the accidents of this drifting Humility, never quite to be extinguished, a few small chances for mercy . . ." (*GR* 610).

Claims that Pynchon's characters are flat or "inadequate to their fictional missions" because they are not shown in the "full complexity and ambiguity of the human social condition" seem, in the light of this analysis, to be inaccurate expressions of discomfort with Pynchon's unusual method of characterization and with his generally self-conscious fictional stance that intentionally distances the reader from the plight of the characters so that their actions may be judged more dispassionately. On one hand, standard patterns of psychological development attest to the consistency of the characters' behavior with patterns of real human behavior. On the other hand, Slothrop and a half dozen other characters in *Gravity's Rainbow* seem to be quite capable of moving any sympathetic reader. I believe that they are fully adequate to their fictional "missions," assuming that the reader comprehends those missions. Pynchon's main concern is not that his characters will bleed when struck, but that the plight of individuals, when examined from psychological, mythological, and (as will be discussed in the next chapter) scientific, mathematical, literary, and philosophical perspectives, will reveal the problems of our time for individuals and communities as well as the possible outcomes of these problems.

4

SOCIO-CULTURAL METAPHORS

Pynchon's ironic detachment from the literary devices he employs (particularly metaphor and analogy) has created a major controversy in the criticism of his work, because it often suggests that the points Pynchon is making through these devices are the opposite of what they seem to be. For instance, Earl Rovit has asserted that the themes of *Gravity's Rainbow* are the "paranoid certainty that everything is causally connected in a sinister" manner and that "the human condition is 'Preterite'"; Rovit's interpretation derives at least in part from his conviction that "gravity's rainbow is the precise metaphorical opposite of God's grace."[1] Yet as my discussion of the von Braun epigraph in my introductory chapter indicates, this kind of simplistic nihilistic interpretation is not an accurate assessment of what Pynchon is attempting, because it forces the reader to leave too much of the novel unaccounted for.

PYNCHON'S USE OF METAPHOR

In the growing volume of writing about Pynchon's works, a critical schism has developed between those who interpret Pynchon's scientific metaphors as objectively reflecting what he thinks is the nature of the universe and those who feel that Pynchon invests the physical sciences with no more authority than he does the literary and mythological systems that he uses in a tentative manner. The narrator sees science itself as composed of metaphorical conceptions of universal forces, and sees metaphorical structures in science, the arts, religion, and even casual figures of speech as all valid but tentative ways of imagining, investigating, and testing the structures of reality. John Leland's conclusion, that "language as a mirror of reality or as a medium capable of establishing significant contacts beyond its own closed system is radically denied in Pynchon's fiction,"[2] is essentially an overreaction to the concern that Pynchon exercises to show the reader that our conceptions of reality must be tentative. We must distrust our language to the extent that we question it, as Emil "Säure" Bummer questions American colloquialisms like "Ass-Backwards." But *Gravity's Rainbow* is quite obviously a search for meaning that does not deny the impossibility of insight through language itself. As in the pragmatism of William James, "universal laws" may be compounded from these hypothetical metaphors of science and language, but they are never more valid than the empirical evidence that gives them momentary substantiation, and must be constantly developed and changed to reflect an apparently fluctuating and barely known reality.

Pynchon uses mythology, the hypothetical constructs of the social sciences, and scientific analogy and metaphor such as those of rocketry, to explain and order the various themes of the novel and to present various possibilities for transcendence or failure within the plot. Beyond explicating the relation of these metaphysical and mytho-poetic structures to plot and theme, and examining some of their specific philosophical implications, I will indicate how the use of archetypes, as discussed by Jung and others, implies both an ambivalence toward natural forces, and a continuing process of life; this counteracts, to a degree, the pessimism of the paranoid characters who dominate the novel.

The root of metaphor is in the structure of the human mind that seeks correspondences among unique phenomena in order to be able to categorize each phenomenon as something generally familiar to the mind. This process of categorizing and generalizing phenomena is often simple and automatic: knowing a few general things about Volkswagens and Fords, one can approximate the danger of stepping in front of a Mercedes at a green light. When correspondences between objects are not so obvious, as those between our sun and the stars are not, for instance, then the mind may first ascribe to an object one or more of the qualities of another that the first object may not possess; this is, by definition, a metaphoric process. The difference between categorizing the automobiles and categorizing the sun as a star or, as Vardaman does in *As I Lay Dying,* as a bloody egg, is not necessarily qualitative but simply involves seeing the correspondences that count in each particular comparison.

Since the nature of subatomic particles and structures and the particulars of the physical laws of the universe are still in doubt, all science is essentially metaphor, however carefully wrought; it is of a kind with mythology, which also seeks to explain the unknown and invisible origins and destinies of man by organizing patterns of correspondences with the known and partially known phenomena of human experience. In *Gravity's Rainbow* the tension between the scientific methods of Pointsman and Mexico exists largely because of Pointsman's insistence that the premise of cause and effect is an absolute universal truth, while Mexico sees it essentially as a metaphor that may have outlived its usefulness for describing a process of correspondences (*GR* 89). Several critics have seen this opposition between Mexico and Pointsman, between a science that recognizes randomness and relativity and one that is completely mechanical and deterministic, as the central tension of the novel. It is not difficult to see that the roles of science and of scientific technology are central to Pynchon's vision of our age, and that understanding this science as both causal agent and metaphor is central to understanding the novel.

One might suspect that whatever controversy might be caused by the applications of Pynchon's scientific metaphors to social systems, at least agreement is possible on the level of what a scientific concept shows about physical reality. This has never been the case with Pynchon. The now famous application of the concept of entropy to civilization is more or less clear in "tenor" (the idea being expressed or the subject of the comparison), but the "vehicle" (the image by which the idea or subject is conveyed) itself casts doubt upon any final interpretation of the metaphor. Henry Adams did not insist that the metaphor of entropy for the breakdown of society was scientific proof that the breakdown would inevitably occur, but merely used the image as a convenience.[3] In *The Crying of Lot 49*, however, Pynchon's apparently more scientific posturing of the concept of entropy has led to a good deal of controversy that affects the interpretation of the key issues of the book. For instance, Peter Abernathy maintains that the novel shows that there is no hope of escaping the "tendency toward entropy in the closed system of America,"[4] while Edward Mendelson shows that the character John Nefastis is scientifically inaccurate in confusing the information theory and the thermodynamic conceptions of entropy.[5] Mendelson claims that Pynchon is not showing a terminal cultural situation and that he is showing that the metaphors of science do not provide objective truths, most obviously because they often conflict with each other in application. Pynchon's self-consciously "paranoid" fiction sees conspiracies and connections where even the average novel might not and then proceeds to cast doubt upon its own constructions where the average novel could not afford to do so. Doubt and suspicion in Pynchon's fiction are inevitably cast on both the appropriateness of the correlation between tenor and vehicle and upon the validity of the vehicle itself. *Gravity's Rainbow* supports the proposition that Pynchon believes that metaphors of science do not provide objective truths, but only relative ones. This novel continually establishes the inadequacy of science to explain natural phenomena, such as Slothrop's erections, by constantly juxtaposing scientific explanations to each other to reveal paradox.

A. N. Whitehead has pointed out that a new—and to many people disturbing—situation in thought has arisen from the fact that scientific theory is rapidly outrunning common sense. Since Newton science had assumed that perception, common sense (including language), and rational thought (including mathematics) faithfully described reality. However, since 1900 particular and quantum physics have provided irrefutable scientific evidence that the world we are familiar with is not what it seems; our minds may not even be suited for comprehending the real nature of space, matter, time, or causality. The new science of Planck and others versus the outmoded positivist science of Newton provides a basic opposition of the forces in the novel; this opposition is expressed through the pair of characters Ned Pointsman and Roger Mexico. As the narrator tells us:

If ever the Antipointsman existed, Roger Mexico is the man. Not so much, the doctor admits, for the psychical research. The young statistician is devoted to number and to method, not table-rapping or wishful thinking. But in the domain of zero to one, not-something to something, Pointsman can only possess the zero and the one. He cannot, like Mexico, survive anyplace in between. Like his master I. P. Pavlov before him, he imagines the cortex of the brain as a mosaic of tiny on/off elements. Some are always in bright excitation, others darkly inhibited. The contours, bright and dark, keep changing. But each point is allowed only the two states: waking or sleep. One or zero. "Summation," "transition," "irradiation," "concentration," "reciprocal induction"—all Pavlovian brain-mechanics—assumes the presence of these bi-stable points. But to Mexico belongs the domain *between* zero and one—the middle Pointsman has excluded from his persuasion—the probabilities. [*GR* 55]

The dichotomy expressed by these characters may also be understood in terms of the mathematical concepts of probabilistic and deterministic models of procedure. The deterministic model, of which Pointsman's stimulus-response charts are an example, postulates that events over time are connected by comprehensible laws in such a manner that unknown situations in either the past or the future may be predicted. Probabilistic models, like Mexico's Poisson distribution, do not claim to predict precise individual occurrences, but describe the probability or possibility of particular outcomes if a particular process is repeated many times. If a process, such as the flipping of a coin, has more than one possible outcome, each outcome has a probability between zero (where the outcome would be impossible) and one (where the outcome is the only possible one). In each particular flip of a coin, there is an equal (50 percent) probability of the coin showing up either heads or tails, and therefore there is no reliable way to predict the outcome of a specific flip. Although it is therefore theoretically possible to flip 100 heads in a row, over the course of 100 flips probabilistic mathematics suggests that we should expect approximately 50 heads and 50 tails.

Pynchon has not assigned his scientists their respective positions arbitrarily; each character represents a complete Weltanschauung. Pointsman cannot live with uncertainty on an emotional or an intellectual level. Like Richard M. Zhluub, he is an obsessive-compulsive personality who seeks to control his environment absolutely: "We must never lose control!" (*GR* 144) he says in reference to the unexplainable and, therefore, perhaps uncontrollable Slothrop. Mexico, however, is able to accept the uncertainties of life, perhaps because he recognizes that uncertainty is an inevitable condition of any existence. Most of the damage Pointsman causes in the novel results from the fact that his compulsion to control increases as it becomes more and more evident that certain matters are uncontrollable. After his attempted castration of Slothrop, motivated almost completely by fear and frustration, Pointsman is cast off by the elect and the preterite and "left only with Cause and Effect, and the rest of his sterile armamentarium" (*GR* 752).

Not only do the two men champion diametrically opposed scientific conceptions of the universe, but they exemplify contrasting psychosexual and emotional makeups as well. Mexico's most obvious characteristic in comparison to the other characters of the novel is his capacity for love, even at the risk of losing that love. We have already seen the importance that the narrator places on Slothrop's inability to love Bianca. Mexico is able to live with uncertainty in both his love for Jessica and the rocket strikes. His Poisson distribution accounts for rocketfalls per area, cavalry accidents, blood counts, radioactive decay, number of wars per year (*GR* 141), as well as the number of babies born during the blitz (*GR* 173). He knows there is an excellent probability that Jessica will go back to Jeremy/Beaver after the war (*GR* 177), but he can live with his hopes of possibility, the realm between zero and one. Pointsman, on the other hand, can only know love as the power of manipulation. What he can control becomes an extension of himself and of his will. Pointsman's desire for human subjects for his experimentation is described in sexual terms: "How Pointsman lusts after them, pretty children. Those drab undershorts of his are full to bursting with need humorlessly, worldly to use their innocence, to write on them new words of himself, his own brown Realpolitik dreams, some psychic prostate ever in aching love promised" (*GR* 50). And later: "'What I want,' Pointsman leaning now into the central radiance of the lamp, his white face more vulnerable than his voice, whispering across the burning spire of a hypodermic set upright on the desk, 'what I really need, is not a dog, not an octopus, but one of your fine Foxes. *Damn it.* One, little, *Fox!*'" (*GR* 52-53). When Pointsman actually finds himself engaged in sex, fellatio calculatingly performed in a closet by Maud Chilkes, he merely wonders if he has found a perfect formula for Christmas punch aphrodisiac: "Try to remember, amphetamine sulphate, 5 mg q 6h, last night amobarbital sodium. . ." (*GR* 168-69).

Important implications of this basic division between Pointsman and Mexico, and between the two forces of deterministic fatalism and of randomness and free will, appear in the mind of the narrator and in the plot and theme of the novel. This division is also carried over into mythological, religious, philosophical, and sociopolitical areas with their attendant metaphorical systems. However, it is important to note that the difference is not between order and chaos, as Pointsman fears when he asks if history, in the hands of Mexico's generation, will be "nothing but events, newly created one moment to the next? No links?" (*GR* 56). Mexico proceeds on patterns that predict the general shape of events rather than the response of a particular subject considered in isolation. Modern mathematical "catastrophe theory" actually seeks to predict the patterns of occurrence of discontinuous phenomena such as "flightfight" and "love-hate" behavior in humans by using three-dimensional geometric figures as models, but, for the mathematician, each particular individual occurrence will still contain a range of probable outcomes, just as in the case of the coin-flipping.

Physiologist-philosopher Ernst Mach pointed out that the idea of cause and effect is in itself an intrusion of the human mind into the domain of nature. The notion of force also projects into the universe, animistically, our own sense of effort or will. Mach wanted to exclude from science terms like "how, because, so, in order to, suppose, as a result, although, and when." The Victorian universe was a machine run by the infallible logic of physics, but this logic is an imposition of the mind or will upon situations that cannot really be known in this way. Chance is not an exceptional or secondary effect in nature, but is inherent in nature and perhaps more operative than cause and effect, since the behavior of individual particles is largely random. Predictability is only probable or possible. Certainty is an abstraction; randomness is the actuality. Pynchon's narrative method differs from that of the followers of Flaubert, who offer the reader very little beyond the empirical data of experience because their style is a reflection of mechanistic philosophy and psychology that posits relationships of stimulus and response but refuses to consider the possibilities of meaning behind these relationships. Camus remarked that the disease of Europe was to believe in nothing and to claim to know everything. Pynchon realizes that we do not know anything without first committing ourselves to a belief in something.

Scientific metaphor in *Gravity's Rainbow* involves an investigation of the nature of the physical (including the spiritual) universe and the relationships of the specific characters to that universe. For instance, the Heisenberg uncertainty principle, which establishes the randomness inherent in nature, can be interpreted on a human level as "legalizing" free will because it maintains that it is not possible to forecast the outcome of any single event. This principle, in itself, requires us to believe in a randomness that may merely be an ignorance of pattern visible, say, to the angels. When Enzian says the Hereros believe that "there is no difference between the behavior of a god and the operations of pure chance" (*GR* 323), he is not denying the possible existence of governing forces but is merely showing his understanding of the fact that humans cannot be aware of any "process of selection" that determines the outcome of individual lives. The Herero name for God, Ndjambi Karunga, is also the name given to sexual intercourse: "To the boy Ndjambi Karunga is what happens when they couple, that's all: God is creator and destroyer, sun and darkness, all sets of opposites brought together, including black and white, male and female. . ." (*GR* 100). The Herero view directly opposes the view of Pynchon's white Protestants, who believe in sacred election and the mechanistic sciences, both of which differentiate rather than integrate human experience and which contribute significantly to an ironclad fatalism that resembles printed circuitry. The battle between the statisticians, anarchists, and organic chemists on one hand, who see life as a freak deviation from the probable that in itself represents the true randomness of nature, and the Pavlovian determinists, inorganic chemists, corporate executives, and military officials on the other, who see everything as controlled, is worked out in the mind of the narrator. He alternately sees everything as tied together within a paranoid vision, as his paranoid history of Lyle Bland indicates (*GR* 580–91), and as random, as the escape of Slothrop and the structuring of various parts of the later narrative indicate. This is the way in which Creative Paranoia functions, at least in part. Pynchon makes the reader aware of the importance of point of view in interpreting empirical data by discussing the "politics of bacteria" (*GR* 4) and Laslo Jamf's "National Socialist chemistry" (*GR* 578). The central metaphor of the novel, "gravity's rainbow," itself suggests the ways in which these points of view, apparently conflicting, intersect in a meaningful way.

GRAVITY'S RAINBOW AND THE ROCKET: MAJOR SCIENTIFIC METAPHORS

The characteristic shape of gravity's rainbow is, of course, the parabola; even when considered as the trajectory of the rocket it

is not only a rocket trajectory, but also a life. You [. . .] "will come to understand that between the points, in the five minutes, *it* lives an entire life. You haven't even learned the data on our side of the flight profile, the visible or trackable. Beyond them there's so much more, so much none of us know. . . ."
But it is a curve each of them feels, unmistakably. It is the parabola. They must have guessed, once or twice—guessed and refused to believe—that everything, always, collectively, had been moving toward that purified shape latent in the sky, that shape of no surprise, no second chances, no return. Yet they do move forever under it, reserved for its own black-and-white bad news certainly as if it were the Rainbow, and they its children. [*GR* 209]

The question of most thematic importance is whether Pynchon means the parabola purely as an indicator of the impossibility of escape from the inevitability of annihilation, as this passage would seem to suggest, or equally as an indicator of the infinite possibility inherent in natural law. There may be no return, but there will be change, transformation, and continuance. The more positive option, continuance, is designated not only by the rainbow's parabola, but also by the rocket, which is represented ambiguously throughout the novel. The flight path of the rocket is

not, as we might imagine, bounded below by the line of the Earth it "rises from" and the Earth it "strikes" No But Then You Never Really Thought It Was Did You Of Course It Begins Infinitely Below The Earth And Goes On Infinitely Back Into The Earth it's only the *peak* that we are allowed to see, the break up through the surface, out of the other silent world. . . . [*GR* 726]

The rocket can be viewed as a supreme technological achievement that affirms only death. Its ascent is "betrayed to Gravity. But," the narrator continues, "the Rocket engine, the deep cry of combustion that is its soul, promises escape. The victim, in bondage to falling, rises on a promise, a prophecy of Escape . . ." (*GR* 758). The rocket may be viewed as a reversal of the process of entropy, a creation of greater order, as "an entire system *won*, away from the feminine darkness, held against the entropies of lovable but scatter-brained Mother Nature" (*GR* 324). In its physical existence the rocket's final disintegration will complete the recapitulation of the fundamental biochemical cycle of life. As the narrator notes in a playful suggestion of the phallic properties of rocket-shaped bananas, the corpses and excrements of dozens of different plants and animals in and around the urban area of London all contribute to the "soil's stringing of rings and chains in nets only God can tell the meshes of, have seen the fruit thrive often to lengths of a foot and a half, yes amazing but true" (*GR* 6).

The reason that "gravity's rainbow" is often interpreted as merely an emblem of limitation and of the ironic "metaphorical opposite of God's grace," is that the continuation of apparently finite processes may exist on the other side of "interfaces," the points at which two worlds touch and are often invisible. As the narrator says, the parabola is "not, as we might imagine, bounded below by the line of the Earth it 'rises from' and the Earth it 'strikes' No . . . It Begins Infinitely Below The Earth And Goes On Infinitely Back Into The Earth it's only the *peak* that we are allowed to see" (*GR* 726).

Because the infinite continuation of the parabola is what Mexico calls "trans-observable," many readers and some of the characters see this continuity as mystical nonsense. But the narrator insists on its possible existence in our daily lives:

Now there grows among all the rooms, replacing the night's old smoke, alcohol and sweat, the fragile, musaceous odor of Breakfast: flowery, permeating, surprising, more than the color of winter sunlight, taking over not so much through any brute pungency or volume as by the high intricacy to the weaving of its molecules, sharing the conjuror's secret by which—though it is not often Death is told so clearly to fuck off—the living genetic chains prove even labyrinthine enough to preserve some human face down ten or twenty generations . . . so the same assertion-through-structure allows this war morning's banana fragrance to meander, repossess, prevail. Is there any reason not to open every window, and let the kind scent blanket all Chelsea? As a spell, against falling objects. . . . [*GR* 10]

Unless the reader is willing to see Prentice's bananas as a kind of gentle phallic procreativity opposing the brutal phallicism of the rocket, he will never be able to accept or fully comprehend the narrator's remarks about death being told "to fuck off." The mystical here is not a different kind of order from physical reality, but merely another manifestation of it. Roger's love for Jessica is another equally mystical phenomenon that is merely unexplainable, not unreal: "In a life he has cursed, again and again, for its need to believe so much in the trans-observable, here is the first, the very first real magic: data he can't argue away" (*GR* 38).

Although I have been considering the rocket and the rainbow as "scientific metaphors," they are obviously interconnected in a number of ways to Pynchon's mythological and social science metaphorical systems. This is due in part to the fact that Pynchon does not use metaphor merely to provide illustrative or tonal parallels to known objects; his metaphorical systems are the means by which the artist, trapped in the tower of his senses, organizes his experience and projects his hypothetical analysis of the unknown.

Pynchon's rocket does not merely represent its metaphoric tonal qualities of phallic power, flight, or destructiveness, but also all of its social, economic, scientific, and historical qualities as vehicle. The "system" of the novel is thus the "system" of the universe, embracing through paradox rather than excluding because of an authorially predetermined pattern. When Pynchon uses science for metaphor, it remains science, but with the full knowledge that science is, after all, a hypothetical construction of reality involving metaphor.

Because of this particular nature of Pynchon's metaphor, the rainbow that is a mark of gravity cannot be written off as ironic metaphor; it is just as likely to be a sign of the interface between our world and another. As Slothrop stands in the gaming room of the Casino Hermann Goering, he

is alone with the paraphernalia of an order whose presence among the ordinary debris of waking he has only lately begun to suspect.
. . . Shortly, unpleasantly so, it will come to him that everything in this room is really being used for something different. Meaning things to Them it has never meant to us. Never. Two orders of being, looking identical . . . but, but . . .

> Oh, THE WORLD OVER THERE, it's
> So hard to explain!
> Just-like, a dream's-got lost in yer brain!
> Dancin' like a fool through the Forbid-den Wing,
> Waitin' fer th' light to start shiver-ing—well,
> Who ev-er said ya couldn't move that way,
> Who ev-er said ya couldn't try?
> If-ya find-there's-a-lit-tle-pain,
> Ya can al-ways-go-back-a-gain, cause
> Ya don't-ev-er-real-ly-say, good-by!

Why here? Why should the rainbow edges of what is almost on him be rippling most intense here in this amply coded room? [*GR* 202-3]

This "other world" that Slothrop seems to enter as he begins to dissolve from the physical world that we inhabit is frequently denoted by the rainbow's promise of transcendence (*GR* 626); Slothrop's "departure" across this rainbow-bridge is quite similar to the departure of Wotan and the gods of Norse mythology, who enter Valhalla for the final time on a rainbow bridge in Wagner's *Twilight of the Gods* after Wotan has betrayed his own design to rescue the world from chaos and, like Slothrop, has become the Wanderer.

MATHEMATICAL IMAGERY

The difficulty of discussing scientific metaphors in isolation from other kinds of metaphor must, by this time, be readily apparent. The image of the parabola that extends infinitely on the other side of an interface leads into the question of transcendence, of its possibility and its shape for humans; these are perhaps the key questions raised in the novel. Pynchon's mathematical imagery in particular suggests an affirmation of the possibility of transcendence.

The quotation from von Braun that appears under the title of the first chapter, "Beyond the Zero," is merely an indication of the centrality of the question of transcendence and transformation. (In mathematics, the apex of a parabola is located at zero.) Von Braun suggests that human life is not merely terminated by death but is somehow transformed and continued "beyond the zero" of death. This concept connects with Leni Pökler's explanation of her transcendence of her fear for her personal safety during a political protest:

> She tried to explain to him about the level you reach, with both feet in, when you lose your fear, you lose it all, you've penetrated the moment, slipping perfectly into its grooves, metal-gray but soft as latex [like the Imipolex shroud that envelopes Gottfried in his final moment of death and/or transcendence], and now the figures are dancing, each pre-choreographed exactly where it is. [...] There is the moment, and its possibilities.
> She even tried, from what little calculus she'd picked up, to explain it to Franz as Δt approaching zero, eternally approaching, the slices of time growing thinner and thinner, a succession of rooms each with walls more silver, transparent, as the pure light of the zero comes nearer....
> [*GR* 158–59]

The Δt image represents the moment in time when personal consequences cease to matter for the protestor because time itself, as duration, no longer exists. When the rocket's trajectory is broken into sections, each an arbitrary Δt in temporal duration, that piece of the trajectory may be examined without reference to time. Δt can never be zero, it can only approach zero as a progressively smaller interval. Leni maintains that at an infinitely small Δt action becomes possible, because when one is locked inside the silver room of the Δt there seems to be no past or future to fear, but only a continual present. Interestingly, her scientist husband, Franz, rebukes her by saying "Δt is just a convenience" (*GR* 159), as he similarly laughs at her for her belief in "parallel systems" of occurrence not governed by cause-and-effect relationships. Like some reviewers of *Gravity's Rainbow*, Franz is unable to appreciate the real connection between science and metaphor. Science and technology have traditionally finessed certain classic problems of philosophy created by its insistence that thought be rational and that intuition is, at best, a poor form of knowledge. The elaboration of a mechanistic or positivist world view depends upon calculus which ignores certain paradoxes such as those of Zeno, which indicate that it is not possible for the mathematician to literalize an infinite number of rates of change (Δts). Calculus simply assigns a term to the infinitesimal instant, the Δt, without comprehending it rationally. This does not solve the philosophical problem, but simply names it and allows us to manipulate the name in order to solve practical problems. Pynchon employs Δt as a symbol of this aspect of reality which we can't understand; it is one of the borderlines of rational knowledge, a compromise with reality, a "reminder of impotence and abstraction."

The Δt image appears later in the novel in conjunction with Slothrop's dispersal; his "temporal bandwidth," the width of his present, "is the familiar 'Δt' considered as a dependent variable" (*GR* 509). Slothrop's loss of temporal bandwidth helps to assure his preterition, his inability to see the significance of the Holy Center of the Rocket, and Δt appears a page later in a similar context:

> But just over the embankment, down in the arena, what might that have been just now, waiting in this broken moonlight, camouflage paint from fins to point crazed into jigsaw . . . is it, then, really never to find you again? Not even in your worst times of night, with pencil words on your page only Δt from the things they stand for? And inside the victim is twitching, fingering beads, touching wood, avoiding any Operational Word. Will it really never come to take you, now? [*GR* 510]

Δt does not correlate directly with transcendence; its appearance signifies the proximity of transcendence just a Δt away, and at the same time reminds us of this infinitesimal margin that somehow must be traversed if we are to attain enlightenment.

Pynchon uses another mathematical symbol, the double integral ($\int\int$), in a number of ways—to suggest the emblem of the SS and the tunnels in the Mittelwerke under Nordhausen, to describe the sleeping forms of lovers, as a symbol for the sun, and in a mathematical procedure to find volume. But, the narrator notes, in the "dynamic space of the living Rocket, the double integral has a different meaning. To integrate here is to operate on a rate of change so that time falls away: change is stilled.... 'Meters per second' will integrate to 'meters.' The moving vehicle is frozen, in space, to become architecture, and timeless. It was never launched. It will never fall" (*GR* 301). This form of integration parallels the function of the Δt, a timelessness within time. However, because the double integral is also used to describe the rocket's "Brennschluss," or end of burning (*GR* 301), it is also a symbol for a kind of death—that is, an end of that part of the rocket's flight that was controlled by man: "A switch closed, fuel cut off, burning ended. The Rocket was on its own" (*GR* 301). Lance Ozier claims: "More appropriately, it was gravity's own. The double integral determined when the Rocket 'died' and was given over to external forces."[6] This point seems convincing because Ozier backs it up by referring to the use of the double integral to signify the death of Klaus Närrisch while he is covering the retreat of Slothrop and von Göll from Peenemünde: "B, B-sub-N-for-Närrisch, is nearly here—nearly about to burn through the last whispering veil to equal 'A'—to equal the only fragment of himself left by them to go through the moment, the irreducible doll of German styrene, shabbier, less authentic than any earlier self . . . a negligible quantity in this last light. . ." (*GR* 518). It rarely pays to rewrite an author's work for purposes of interpretation, but Ozier seems to be correct in his assertion that "the process of double integration that calculates the fatal B_n is like a transformation of life into death as well as a transformation of time into eternity."[7] Pynchon's initial discussion of the rocket's Brennschluss occurs in a passage of general commentary on the double integral sign (*GR* 299–302) that includes references to its "backward symmetry . . . that Pointsman missed, but Katje didn't. 'A life of its own,' she said" (*GR* 301). Pynchon does not say "gravity's own," as Ozier suggests he might, because Pynchon is playing off the fact that the rocket is controlled by humans who are aware of its flight path, while the rocket itself is only aware of its own rate of acceleration. This is important as a parallel to Slothrop, who is aware of the furious activity of his life without being able to see the direction toward which They are manipulating him. In this sense, the rocket and Slothrop have a certain amount of freedom only after their official deaths—that is, beyond the zero of Their control. This is a fact that the narrator wishes to emphasize, and he does so immediately:

That is one meaning of the shape of the tunnels down here in the Mittelwerke. Another may be the ancient rune that stands for the yew tree, or Death. The double integral stood in Etzel Olsch's subconscious

for the method of finding hidden centers, inertias unknown, as if mono-
liths had been left for him in the twilight, left behind by some corrupted
idea of "civilization," in which eagles cast in concrete stand ten meters
high at the corners of the stadiums where the people, a corrupted idea
of "the People" are gathering, in which birds do not fly, in which imaginary centers far down inside the solid fatality of stone are thought
of not as "heart," "plexus," "consciousness," (the voice speaking here
grows more ironic, closer to tears which are not all theatre, as the list
goes on . . .) "Sanctuary," "dream of motion," "cyst of the eternal present," or "Gravity's gray eminence among the councils of living stone."
No, as none of these, but instead a point in space, a point hung precise
as the point where burning must end, never launched, never to fall. And
what is the specific shape whose center of gravity is the Brennschluss
Point? Don't jump at an infinite number of possible shapes. There's only
one. It is most likely an interface between one order of things and
another. There's a Brennschluss point for every firing site. They still
hang up there, all of them, a constellation waiting to have a 13th sign
of the Zodiac named for it . . . but they lie so close to Earth that from
many places they can't be seen at all, and from different places inside
the zone where they can be seen, they fall into completely different
patterns. . . . [GR 302]

The specific shape of this "interface between one order of things and
another" is apparently a parabola, because its "center of gravity" is
a close parallel here to the Holy Center of the Rocket and ultimately
suggests that at the very heart of the physical laws of the universe, at
the evergreen yew tree that was the center of the Norse mythological
universe, connecting the worlds of the living and the dead, of gods and
mortals, and at the very point of death itself (as Kabbalist Steve Edelman
says, the Bodenplatte, "the delta-t itself" [GR 754]), lies an interface
between forms of existence that allows transcendence into a new form
of being. God's rainbow promised that the next form of death would also
be a form of transcendence—at least according to Cardinal Spellman and
the bishops of the United States.

The narrator of *Gravity's Rainbow* continually relates the concepts
of the delta-t, interface, and "singularity" (the infinitesimal point at which
something ends and something else—or nothing else—begins) to transformation from one form of existence, physical or spiritual, to another
form. But the Polish undertaker who goes out in his rowboat in hopes
of being hit by lightning and thus "enlightened," parodies the application of these same concepts:

Well, it's a manner of continuity. Most people's lives have ups and
downs that are relatively gradual, a sinuous curve with first derivatives at
every point. They're the ones who never get struck by lightning. No
real idea of cataclysm at all. But the ones who do get hit experience a

singular point, a discontinuity in the curve of life—do you know what the time rate of change *is* at a cusp? *Infinity,* that's what! A-and right across the point, it's *minus* infinity! How's *that* for sudden change, eh? Infinite miles per hour changing to the same speed *in reverse,* all in a gnat's-ass or red cunt hair of the Δt across the point. That's getting hit by lightning, folks. You're *way* up there on the needle-peak of a mountain, and don't think there aren't lammergeiers cruising there in the lurid red altitudes around, waiting for a chance to snatch you off. Oh yes. They are piloted by bareback dwarves with little plastic masks around their eyes that happen to be shaped just like the infinity symbol: ∞. Little men with wicked eyebrows, pointed ears and bald heads, although some of them are wearing outlandish headgear, not at all the usual Robin Hood fedoras, no these are *Carmen Miranda* hats, for example, bananas, papayas, bunches of grapes, pears, pineapples, mangoes, jeepers even *watermelons*—and there are World War I spike-top Wilhelmets, and baby bonnets and crosswise Napoleon hats with and without the Ns on them, not to mention little red suits and green capes, well here they are leaning forward into their cruel birds' ears, whispering like jockeys, out to nab you, buster, just like that sacrificial ape off of the Empire State building, except that they won't let you fall, they'll carry you away, to the places they are agents of. It will *look* like the world you left, but it'll be different. Ha-*ha!* But the lightning-struck know, all right! Even if they may not *know* they know. And that's what this undertaker tonight has set out into the storm to find. [*GR* 664]

Near the end of the novel the narrator employs the concept of singularity to parody the inability of Pointsman and his old-fashioned company to accept the "new dispensation" that marks the beginning of man's transformation:

At long last, after a distinguished career of uttering, "My God, we are too late!" always with the trace of a sneer, a pro-forma condescension—because of course he *never* arrives too late, there's always a reprieve, a mistake by one of the Yellow Adversary's hired bunglers, at worst a vital clue to be found next to the body—now, finally, Sir Denis Nayland Smith *will* arrive, my God, too late.

Superman will swoop boots-first into a deserted clearing, a launcher-erector sighing oil through a slow seal-leak, gum evoked from the trees, bitter manna for this bitterest of passages. The colors of his cape will wilt in the afternoon sun, curls on his head begin to show their first threads of gray. [. . .]

"Too late" was never in their programming. They find instead a moment's suspending of their sanity—but then it's over with, whew, and it's back to the trail, back to the *Daily Planet.* Yes, Jimmy, it *must've been the day I ran into the singularity, those few seconds of absolute mystery . . . you know Jimmy, time—time is a funny thing. . . .* There'll be a thousand ways to forget. The heroes will go on, kicked upstairs to oversee the development of bright new middle-line personnel, and they will watch their system falling apart, watch those singularities begin to come more and more often, proclaiming another dispensation out of the old-fashioned time, and they'll call it cancer, and just won't know what things are coming to, or what's the meaning of it all, Jimmy.... [*GR* 751-52]

The narrator depicts transformation in a number of ways that we will continue to examine: for Leni Pökler and Slothrop, transformation involves a radical loss of self, not unlike Martin Buber's conception of what must happen in the transcendence into mutual being between a person and someone or something else in an "I-Thou" relationship; Buber's I-Thou relationship is itself an interface between the world that creates our sense of self and the self that creates its world. "The It-world coheres in space and time. The Thou-world does not cohere in either. It coheres in the center in which the extended lines of relationships intersect in the eternal Thou."[8] Buber describes the I-Thou relationship as an unmediated state in which "nothing conceptual intervenes between I and [Thou], no prior knowledge and no imagination; and memory itself is changed as it plunges from particularity into wholeness."[9] The world of the It is the public world of manipulation, of use and causality, and Buber finds it a necessary part of life because the ability to experience and use comes about through that part of man's life. Man must be both physical and spiritual to be complete. The man to whom

freedom is guaranteed does not feel oppressed by causality. He knows that his mortal life is by its very nature an oscillation between ... [Thou] and It, and he senses the meaning of this. It suffices him that again and again he may set foot on the threshold of the sanctuary in which he could never tarry. Indeed, having to leave it again and again is for him an intimate part of the meaning and destiny of his life.[10]

On the one hand, Slothrop's disintegration can be seen as a total transcendence of his human state—he does not merely set foot on the interface, but crosses over into the realm of spirit where there are no borders between subject and object. On the other hand, Slothrop has abandoned his ability to manipulate anything in the physical world and has abdicated his rocket quest to revitalize the world of It.

It is not clear whether the narrator believes transcendence from one world order or one state of being into others, to be inevitable; however, his use of mathematical and scientific imagery—of the Δt, the double integral, and the singular point—coupled with analogous systems in religion, the arts, and mythology, strongly suggests the possibility. Pynchon does not define the potential of these transcendent realms very clearly, but he does suggest that they are grounded in the world we know and are therefore not purely chaotic or formless.

The problem with applying mathematical imagery to human life is simply that mathematics is an abstract system of patterns without content beyond the McLuhanesque substance of "medium as message." Mathematical imagery may give us some of the tools for deciphering reality, but reality itself remains only a potential shape. We do not know specifically from these analogies what transcendence means in human terms. This imagery must be coupled with other analogous systems of the novel, such as Buber's ontologies, in order to clarify the meaning of Pynchon's construction. James Earl points out that

in this Wonderland of the physicist, the mysterious obedience of events in large numbers to laws like Mexico's Poisson equation leads us to principles of order and symmetry in the universe which are themselves beyond the reach of rational analysis. Man has always suspected the existence of such principles, and has given many names to his suspicions. All the supernatural elements in the *Rainbow* can be interpreted in terms of this dualism, between the order we perceive in the world, and our intuition of greater, invisible, and incomprehensible forces, which give us the sense of haunting and unaccountable structures in history.[11]

LITERARY ANALOGY

What might be considered the opposite end of the metaphoric spectrum, literary analogy, actually presents the set of concepts most complementary to Pynchon's scientific metaphors. The poetry of Rainer Maria Rilke has been recognized by almost every reader to be the most important such reference in *Gravity's Rainbow,* although many critics seem to have misunderstood *Sonnets to Orpheus* and *Duino Elegies* in applying them to the novel. These works are not the doom songs of western civilization, but depict the struggle of the human spirit to transcend its mortal restraints. Rilke has called the theme of the *Sonnets* "the will to metamorphosis."[12]

The opening line of *Gravity's Rainbow,* "A screaming comes across the sky," is frequently compared to the opening line of the *Elegies,* "Who, if I cried, would hear me among the angelic orders?"[13] In this context, Pynchon's novel is his cry for an answer to questions similar to the ones asked by Rilke in the *Elegies.* (Critics who read *Gravity's Rainbow* as apocalyptically nihilistic twist this line around to suggest that the screaming of the Rocket is the answer of the Angels to man, but the Angels remain aloof in both the poems and the novel, and I do not see any direct way to arrive at this conclusion without torturing both texts.) The *Elegies* were a turning point in Rilke's career; previously he had struggled "from outward forms to win / The passion and the life, whose fountains are within." In the *Elegies,* like Pynchon in *Gravity's Rainbow,* he wanted to fashion, as J. B. Leishman says, "some ultimate vision of human life and destiny and of the true relationship between the looker and that world on which he had looked so intensely."[14]

Rilke regarded external phenomena as symbols of spiritual experience; "The Angel of the Elegies," Rilke wrote, "is the creature in whom that transformation of the visible into the invisible we are performing already appears complete. . . . The Angel of the Elegies is the being who vouches for the recognition of a higher degree of reality in the invisible—therefore 'terrible' to us, because we, its lovers and transformers, still depend on the visible."[15] Leishman describes Rilke's Angel as "a being in whom the limitations and contradictions of present human nature have been transcended, a being in whom thought and action, insight and achievement, will and capability, the actual and the ideal, are one."[16] Pynchon refers to his Angels as having similar properties, such as the ability to make precise predictions of particular occurrences from the Poisson distribution that are beyond the present sphere of human knowledge. Both Rilke and Pynchon's narrator fear that the Angels may be merely using humanity as a lower form of life; the *Elegies* are a lament for the limitations of mankind in this sense. In the "Eighth Elegy," Leishman notes, Rilke

insists upon a still more fundamental defect or limitation—the fact that in almost all consciousness there is a distinction between what philosophers call subject and object: the fact that our awareness of Being, or existence, as an object, as something distinct from ourselves, prevents us from identifying ourselves with it and achieving a condition of pure Being or pure existence. Being or existence perceived as something not-ourselves, Rilke calls "World," and contrasts with what he calls "the open," "the nowhere without no." In this "open" world there is no time, no past or future, no end, no limit, no separation or parting, and no death as the opposite of life.[17]

The similarity between Rilke's "condition of pure Being" and Buber's I-Thou relationship is particularly striking in light of Slothrop's dispersal, which involves the loss of ego and unification with nature (*GR* 626). In fact, Slothrop comes closest to being "a spiritual medium" when he listens to what "that Rilke prophesied" in *Sonnets to Orpheus:*

> And though Earthliness forget you,
> To the stilled Earth say: I flow.
> To the rushing water speak: I am. [*GR* 622]

Eventually, in the "Ninth Elegy," Rilke answers his earlier fears concerning the angels' manipulation of mankind by asserting that if we submit to their powers we will be uplifted or at least well used. He repeated this idea in the *Sonnets:*

> Spectre of mortal fragility,
> simply-receptive docility
> smiles when your shadow descends.
>
> We can be, with our waxing and waning,
> fitlier used by remaining
> forces for ultimate ends.[18]

The ultimate triumph of the *Elegies* that is celebrated in the *Sonnets* is man's triumph over death by his submission to it; man will transcend through the loss of the temporally limited self and achieve a spiritual transformation through unity with the earth. As the "Ninth Elegy" says,

> . . . Earth! invisible!
> What is your urgent command, if not transformation?
> . . . .
> You were always right, and your holiest inspiration's
> Death, that friendly Death.
> Look, I am living. On what? Neither childhood nor future
> are growing less. . . . Supernumerous existence wells up in my heart.

As the young man of the *Elegies* approaches the mountains of Primal Pain, he looks down into a gorge,

> where it gleams in the moonlight,—
> there, the source of Joy. With awe
> she names it, says "Among men
> it's a carrying stream."

As Slothrop fails to recognize the Holy Center of the Rocket at Peenemünde, the narrator asks:

> But just over the embankment, down in the arena, what might that have been just now, waiting in this broken moonlight, camouflage paint from fins to point crazed into jigsaw . . . is it, then, really never to find you again? Not even in your worst times of night, with pencil words on your page only Δt from the things they stand for? . . . avoiding any Operational Word. Will it really never come to take you, now? (*GR* 510)

Unlike the young woman, Slothrop can neither recognize the source of "Joy" embodied in this vision of the Rocket nor "name it," and therefore he cannot make this "carrying stream" a conscious part of himself. But Slothrop does regain his harp and does seem to achieve the final state of grace that, as Rilke says, is not happiness, but "the emotion that almost startles / when happiness falls."

The conditions of transformation in the *Elegies* describe Slothrop's dissolution more precisely than any of the other systems of analogy employed by Pynchon: Slothrop loses his ego, enters into a certain timeless state, reaches harmony with the earth, and becomes invisible as he apparently approaches both a state of grace and "a weird death" (*GR* 742).

The "Tenth Elegy," Weissmann's favorite (*GR* 98), is an affirmation of suffering and pain as "our winter foliage, our sombre evergreen, *one* / of the seasons of our interior year." Like the evergreen yew tree to which Pynchon compares the rocket (*GR* 754), man can be seen as surviving, transformed through the pain of death to a new form of being. Blicero, as the man of destiny approaching the Mountains of Primal Pain, believes himself to be rushing toward transformation in his rush toward death.

But not all forms of pain and death are necessarily good in Rilke's mind. In this same elegy, the "Tenth," he satirizes the dwellers of "The City of Pain,"

> where, in the seeming stillness of uproar outroared,
> stoutly, a thing cast out from the mould of vacuity,
> swaggers that gilded fuss, the bursting memorial.
> How an Angel would tread beyond trace their market of comfort,
> with the church alongside, bought ready for use: as clean
> and disenchanted and shut as the Post on a Sunday!
> Outside, though, there's always the billowing edge of the fair.
> Swings of Freedom! Divers and Jugglers of Zeal!
> . . . .
>   Cheer-struck, on he goes reeling
> after his luck. For booths that can please
> the most curious tastes are drumming and bawling.
>   Especially
> worth seeing (for adults only): the breeding of Money!
> Anatomy made amusing! Money's organs on view!
> Nothing concealed!

This is the world in which Pointsman believes and which They seem to promote—perhaps as a disguise for something else. Rilke's system of transcendence, while obviously imitated in *Gravity's Rainbow,* is just one more of the possibilities that the narrator sees. If he was sure of the particulars of this transformation, he would probably align himself more clearly and unconditionally with Blicero. As Närrisch is waiting to be killed, the narrator poses the possible comfort of Rilkean transformation, but this eludes Närrisch, to whom death appears only as a hard, gunmetal fact:

He's forgotten its ending, the last Rilke-elegiac shot of weary Death leading the two lovers away hand in hand through the forget-me-nots. No help at all from that quarter. Tonight Närrisch is down to the last tommy-gun of his career, foreign and overheated . . . and blisters on his hands he won't have to worry about tomorrow. No sources of mercy available beyond the hard weapon, the burning fingers—a cruel way to go out. (*GR* 516]

Furthermore, the pattern of this system of metaphor that depicts Slothrop as "saved" conflicts with the narrator's other evaluation of Slothrop as a "passed-over" Tannhäuser, also a well-developed analogy. Finally, the narrator cannot be sure that every form of transformation is positive; for instance, when Jamf preaches his Nazi chemistry, he says "move beyond life, toward the inorganic. Here is no fragility, no mortality—here is Strength, and the Timeless" (*GR* 580). The insignium of this particular concept is "Si-N," and Slothrop is constantly aware that They are using him for "something" that is "somehow" evil. The angels may not even be the same as They after all; but Rilke's transcendence is a possibility among the alternative patterns with which the narrator describes his world.

TECHNOLOGY AS METAPHOR FOR MAN'S ACHIEVEMENTS

The narrator's attitude toward technology itself is a good deal more ambivalent than his scientific and mathematical or his literary imagery; this is probably because, as the rocket shows, technology can be used for either good or bad ends. In this sense, technology exemplifies the same ambivalence as phallic potency or any other force that man might use to realize designs that may be either good or bad. The Δt, itself a symbol for a means of transcendence, becomes in its technological application a device for perpetrating the "pornography of flight" and the fragmentation of sensibility. Many readers claim that technology in

Gravity's Rainbow ultimately absorbs and debases all that was potentially inspiriting in its discovery. To support this view, some critics cite the dream of Kekulé von Stradonitz which the narrator suggests "made the IG possible" (*GR* 410):

> Kekulé dreams the Great Serpent holding its own tail in its mouth, the dreaming Serpent which surrounds the World. But the meanness, the cynicism with which the dream is to be used. The Serpent that announces, "The World is a closed thing, cyclical, resonant, eternally-returning," is to be delivered into a system whose only aim is to *violate* the Cycle. Taking and not giving back, demanding that "productivity" and "earnings" keep on increasing with time, the System removing from the rest of the World these vast quantities of energy to keep its own tiny desperate fraction showing a profit: and not only most of humanity—most of the World, animal, vegetable and mineral, is laid waste in the process. The System may or may not understand that it's only buying time. And that time is an artificial resource to begin with, of no value to anyone or anything but the System, which sooner or later must crash to its death, when its addiction to energy has become more than the rest of the World can supply, dragging with it innocent souls all along the chain of life. [*GR* 412]

Joseph Slade, on the other hand, believes that World War II released the new "charismatic energies" of "the Second Industrial Revolution." Technological energies, he says, are not linear but cyclical and potentially disruptive to rationalized systems of control such as They employ. Slade does not elaborate much, but he is apparently referring to concepts of Marshall McLuhan's, whose influence on Pynchon is attested to by a letter that Pynchon wrote.[19] McLuhan points out that every culture and every age has its favorite model of perception and knowledge that it is inclined to prescribe for everybody and everything. Electric technology, he maintains, is at least partially responsible for our contemporary aspirations for wholeness, empathy, and depth of awareness, and for a revulsion against imposed patterns. Man becomes more integrated and completed by electronic technology that extends his senses: according to McLuhan, our central nervous system itself has been extended in a global embrace, abolishing both space and time on our planet.[20] This is the opposite effect of the mechanistic analysis spawned by Victorian industrialism, which, like the "pornography" of calculus, breaks things down into isolated components; this manner of perceiving the world is, as Blicero remarks, "Europe's Original Sin" (*GR* 722).

Technology, then, may become the great connector of men, or it may become the ultimate means for their subjugation and control. Enzian is only one of a number of characters who imagine that World War II was never political at all, the politics was all theatre, all just to keep the people distracted . . . secretly, it was being dictated instead by the needs of technology . . . by a conspiracy between human beings and techniques, by something that needed the energy-burst of war, crying, "Money be damned, the very life of [insert name of Nation] is at stake," but meaning, most likely, *dawn is nearly here, I need my night's blood, my funding, funding, ahh more, more.* . . . The real crises were crises of allocation and priority, not among firms—it was only staged to look that way—but among the different Technologies, Plastics, Electronics, Aircraft, and their needs which are understood only by the ruling elite. . . .

Yes but Technology only responds (how often this argument has been iterated, dogged and humorless as a Gaussian reduction, among the younger Schwarzkommando especially), "All very well to talk about having a monster by the tail, but do you think we'd've had the Rocket if someone, some specific somebody with a name and a penis hadn't *wanted* to chuck a ton of Amatol 300 miles and blow up a block full of civilians? Go ahead, capitalize the T on technology, deify it if it will make you feel less responsible—but it puts you in the neutered, brother, in with the eunuchs keeping the harem of our stolen Earth for the numb and joyless hardons of human sultans, human elite with no right at all to be where they are—"

We have to look for power sources here, and distribution networks we were never taught, routes of power our teachers never imagined, or were encouraged to avoid [. . .] trying to learn the real function . . . zeroing in on what incalculable plot? Up here, on the surface, coal-tars, hydrogenation, synthesis were always phony, dummy functions to hide the real, the *planetary mission* yes perhaps centuries in the unrolling . . . this ruinous plant, waiting for its Kabbalists and new alchemists to discover the Key, teach the mysteries to others. . . . [*GR* 521]

Enzian fears, but ultimately rejects, the possibility that man cannot escape the clutches of technological forces that might subvert his transcendence into what Blicero calls a "cycle of infection and death" (*GR* 724). The spirit of Walter Rathenau, organizer of the German corporate state, advances the theory that what we have come to regard as the natural cycle of organic life is really only a symbolic "impersonation of life."

"The real movement is not from death to any rebirth. It is from death to death-transfigured.

". . . You think you'd rather hear about what you call 'life': the growing, organic Kartell. But it's only another illusion. A very clever robot. The more dynamic it seems to you, the more deep and dead, in reality, it grows. Look at the smokestacks, how they proliferate, fanning the wastes of original wastes over greater and greater masses of city. [. . .] The persistence, then, of structures favoring death. Death converted into more death. Perfecting its reign, just as the buried coal grows denser, and overlaid with more strata—epoch on top of epoch, city on top of ruined city. This is the sign of Death the impersonator.

"These signs are real. They are also symptoms of a process. The process follows the same form, the same structure. To apprehend it you will follow the signs. All talk of cause and effect is secular history, and secular history is a diversionary tactic. [. . .]

"You must ask two questions. First, what is the real nature of synthesis? And then: what is the real nature of control?

"You think you know, you cling to your beliefs. But sooner or later you will have to let them go. . . ." [*GR* 166-67]

Rathenau's statement gives shape to some of Their designs. It describes a form of anti-transcendence, one more possible result of man's technological achievements.

SOCIAL SCIENCE AS METAPHOR / METAPHOR AS SOCIAL SCIENCE

The elective affinity of the economics and technology of our time for systems of greater control is expressed in *Gravity's Rainbow* through references to the sociology of Max Weber. Because he is examining society, Pynchon employs Weber's sociology both directly—coupling it with other metaphor—and indirectly—as a metaphorical system that suggests suprasocial phenomena. It should be noted that Weber himself was essentially a positivist who scorned "philosophical" or "metaphysical" elements in the social sciences. Like Marx, Weber formulated his concept of the "state" in terms of a "monopoly of the use of legitimate force over a given territory," but he replaced the central dynamic of the Marxian system—class struggle—with a variety of political and economic concerns. For Weber, the contemporary shape of these forces was realized most efficiently in modern capitalism, as institutionalized in the "rational" bureaucracies of state and industry that could best promote efficiency of production, continuity of operation, speed, precision, and the calculation of results. Capitalism has created the system of values, termed by Weber "the Protestant ethic," that optimizes the adaptability of man to bureaucracy. Paradoxically, Weber classed himself as a "liberal" whose future was doomed by the very system he predicted. Because bureaucracy was the logical outcome of the sociological process, he identified it as "rationality," the logical self-perpetuation of what might almost be described as a viral system mindlessly reproducing itself; he identified the process of rationalization with mechanism, depersonalization, and oppressive routine, and noted that, in this context, rationality is adverse to personal freedom.

The extent and direction of rationalization in the world can be measured negatively by the disappearance of "magical elements of thought" (which include the justifications for humanism). It can be measured positively according to the gain in systematic coherence. Weber used a phrase from Schiller to describe this process of rationalization as "'the disenchantment of the world.'" The concept can be extended to any part of the culture, including, for instance, music. Weber perceived the following as part of this process: the fixation of "clang patterns"; the establishment of a well-tempered scale due to more precise notation; "harmonious" tonal music; and the standardization of certain woodwinds and string instruments as the core of the symphony orchestra. (Remember, the narrator of *Gravity's Rainbow* depicts the progressive dislocations of jazz as a willful reversal of this process on the part of black musicians.)

In 1906 Weber said that the opportunities for democracy and individualism looked very bad from the standpoint of "the lawful effects of material interests." The development of these interests, Weber declared, pointed directly in the opposite direction: to "benevolent feudalism" in America, to "welfare institutions" in Germany, and to the collective life in Russia. Weber concluded that "everywhere the house is ready-made for a new servitude."[21]

However, again unlike Marx, Weber did not believe that any system is utterly inevitable. The process of rationalization may be reversed by certain discontinuities in history, phenomena that Pynchon might call singularities. When routine forms of life prove insufficient for controlling a growing state of tension, stress, or suffering, institutional structures may disintegrate, allowing the rise of a new order, possibly under the auspices of a "charismatic" leader, who will be followed by those in need who believe him to be extraordinarily gifted. ("Charisma" literally means "gift of grace.") Weber describes the charismatic leader in terms that can be applied in part, but not in whole, to Slothrop, Weissmann, Enzian, and to the rocket itself: miracles, revelations, heroic feats of valor, and baffling success are characteristic marks of the leaders of this stature, while any failure marks their immediate ruin. Christ, Buddha, Napoleon, and Hitler are all appropriate examples of the archetypal charismatic leader. Weber sees them as truly revolutionary forces in history. Charisma—which thrives on personality and personal interaction, spontaneity, inner freedom, creativity, and imaginative flights of genius—clearly opposes the rationalizations of bureaucracy, which promote institutions and depersonalization, routine, conventionality, rules, and drudgery. Unfortunately, the genuine charismatic situation must quickly give way to incipient institutions; as the original doctrines are democratized, they are intellectually adjusted to the needs of the stratum which is the primary carrier of the leader's message. During the "routinization of charisma" the material interests of the evolving power base are the most compelling factor.

Weber summed up the long-run influence of "ideas" by maintaining: "Not ideas, but material and ideal interests directly govern man's conduct. Yet very frequently the 'world images' which have been created by 'ideas' have, like switchmen, determined the tracks along which action has been pushed by the dynamic of interests."[22] Weber felt that freedom consisted not in realizing alleged historical necessities, but in making deliberate choices between open alternatives. The possibilities of the future are not infinite and are not easily malleable, yet there is room for the strategies of such a group as the Counterforce. As a charismatic leader who might have changed the course of history, Slothrop is obviously a failure. Even Blicero, whom Enzian describes quite specifically as a charismatic leader, suffers the routinization of his ideology after his disappearance (*GR* 325).

Essentially, then, the narrator's analogies with Weber's sociology are more pessimistic than his scientific metaphors, yet are not totally hopeless. "They" misinterpret Weber's concepts on purpose in order to make charisma disreputable as the "terrible disease" that spawned World War II (*GR* 81). Thanatz apparently sees the rocket's charisma as effective merely in switching the destructive impulses of western civilization onto a particular technological track (*GR* 464), but then he is a sadomasochist. In any event, the rocket's charisma will be routinized and turned to Their use, since no one else seems willing or able to use it.

Pynchon follows Weber in associating the rationalizing processes of bureaucracy with the religious and cultural doctrines of Calvinism, a religion that equates ultimate (spiritual) success with material success. Throughout *Gravity's Rainbow* Calvinism is generally portrayed as a repressive system of values because it is fatalistic and predicates submission to destiny—a future that actually may not be as inevitable as They want everyone to believe. Slothrop's Calvinist background is at least partly responsible for his sensitivity to signs and patterns, but many critics have seized upon the narrator's use of the terminology of "preterition" and "election" to oversimplify Pynchon's conception of the world in the novel. Scott Sanders, for instance, maintains that, "if elect, one's life is filled with meaning, because one is incorporated into God's scheme of salvation. If preterite, one's life is meaningless, not so much damned as simply void, because one is excluded from God's plan. These are exactly the binary possibilities imagined by Pynchon."[23] Calvinism is one of the metaphorical systems for describing the world that the narrator considers, but we have already seen enough of the complexity of the narrator's vision to dismiss this argument as simplistic. Mexico, for instance, scoffs at Pointsman's insistence on "binary possibilities." But Sanders raises several objections to what he sees to be Pynchon's oversimplification of the world. Sanders schematizes the parallels between Pynchon and Puritanism in a particularly reductive manner:

Pynchon	Puritanism
paranoia	faith
cosmic conspiracy	God's plan
Gravity	God's will
membership in the Firm	election
exclusion from conspiracy	preterition
multiple narrative patterns	typology
remote control	grace
binary vision	theism/atheism
decadence of history	depravity of man
paranoid self-reference	personal salvation
the Zero	Last Judgment[24]

Sanders brutalizes archetypal concepts in both columns of this comparison. Jungian archetypes are not inherently good or bad, but merely important. All individuals attribute qualities to the archetypes that differentiate their meanings, but because archetypes represent natural forces in both the internal and the external worlds, they will always reflect the positive or negative experiences of individuals with essentially ambivalent forces. Nor is the human response to these "complexes" likely to be simple. Like the archetypes that are so important in Wagner's operas, the significance of every important symbol in *Gravity's Rainbow* is ultimately ambiguous.[25]

RELIGION AS METAPHOR, METAPHOR AS RELIGION

An adequate understanding of religion and of the metaphorical functioning of religion and mythology is necessary to a full realization of what Pynchon has created in *Gravity's Rainbow*. According to Mircea Eliade, our sense of this function has atrophied because modern man, following the principles of positivism, has tried to abolish any form of the inexplicable and to regard himself as a purely historical being in a mechanistic cosmos. This assertion is, of course, similar to Weber's description of industrialized society. And Calvinism, with its fatalistic discouragement of any attempt to comprehend the sacred, essentially amounts to a philosophy of materialistic determinism. Calvinism itself has been a "desacralizing" force. On the other hand, Slothrop's propensity to look for "signs" is really a healthy release of a repressed human tendency back toward the truly sacred. Many of Slothrop's ancestors were branded heretics by the other Puritans for having this same tendency. Eliade notes that Marxism and depth psychology illustrate the effectiveness of "demystification" when one wants to discover the true or original significance of a behavior, an action, or a cultural creation. Eliade maintains that we have to apply the same process to modern art in order to discover the sacred elements in an apparently abstract or "profane" painting.[26] Benny Profane of *V.* is Pynchon's example of a contemporary who refuses to recognize the sacred in his world—and is doomed by his refusal.

But the sacred is an element in the structure of human consciousness, not a stage in the history of consciousness, and it cannot be repressed indefinitely. The nihilism that flourished in the first half of this century in the arts of western civilization was a response to the complete lack of unconditional values of the kind that religion has traditionally supplied. According to Eliade, life becomes meaningful through the imitation of paradigmatic models revealed by transhuman phenomena, initially known to men simply as supernatural beings. For Eliade, the study of religion involves the development of a "competent hermeneutics" to investigate "hierophanies," the manifestations of the sacred expressed in symbols, rituals, and myths that are actually "messages" to be deciphered and understood. The narrator in *Gravity's Rainbow* is attempting to construct just such a hermeneutics for the investigation of the hierophanies of our modern world.

According to Eliade, every religion has a central conception or symbol, called a "cosmic object." However, it is not the object itself that is venerated, but the sacred that is manifested through the object. The narrator of *Gravity's Rainbow* makes several suggestions that the rocket is such an object. A religious system begins when a series of myths coalesce into a mythology called a "cosmogonic myth" that tells symbolically the story of the creation of the world and of man's relationship to the world. The reference point of "creation," which Eliade calls "the Time of the Myths," is concurrent with the period when man's essential nature was determined, as in the "assembly" of Slothrop's time during World War II. The cosmogonic myth reveals the creation of the world and of man and, at the same time, the principles that govern the cosmic process and human existence. Myths succeed each other and form themselves into a sacred history which is continuously recovered in the life of the community as well as in the life of each individual, because what happened in the beginning describes both the original perfection and the destiny of each individual. The cosmogonic myth and its sequels reveal the structures of reality and of the individual's proper mode of being.[27]

Eliade says that the rediscovery of the sacred is the rediscovery of life and nature, of a sense of unity with the earth itself. Lyle Bland, who has made that rediscovery, has a hard time getting over the wonder of finding that Earth is a living critter, after all these years of thinking about a big dumb rock to find a body and psyche, he feels like a child again, he knows that in theory he must not attach himself, but still he is in love with his sense of wonder, with having found it again, even this late, even knowing he must soon let it go. . . . To find that Gravity, taken so for granted, is really something eerie, Messianic, extrasensory in Earth's mindbody . . . having hugged to its holy center the wastes of dead species, gathered, packed, transmuted, realigned, and rewoven molecules to be taken up again by the coal-tar Kabbalists of the other side, the ones Bland on his voyages has noted, taken boiled off, teased apart, explicated to every last permutation of useful magic, centuries past exhaustion still finding new molecular pieces, combining and recombining them into new synthetics. . . . [GR 590]

The Hereros' firing of their 00001 is apparently a ritual repetition of Blicero's firing for the purpose of mythically revitalizing their world. Because the new order is expected to rise out of chaos, and new life to rise out of death, Enzian himself may be the ritual sacrifice recapitulating the role of Gottfried in the rocket nose. Within the structure of the novel Pynchon indicates this relationship between the two rockets by chronologically leading up to the firing of the 00001 and then depicting instead the firing of Blicero's original 00000.

The pattern of Pynchon's cosmogonic myth will be examined in the final chapters of this study, but the significance of the narrator's continual application of religious and mystic terminology to people, places, and events in the novel should now be clear. The myth itself will remain incomplete, perhaps because it has not completely coalesced for our culture, or perhaps because, as the narrator fears, our guide is ranked among the preterite and is without the knowledge of a Lyle Bland:

The rest of us, not chosen for enlightenment, left on the outside of Earth, at the mercy of a Gravity we have only begun to learn how to detect and measure, must go on blundering inside our front-brain faith in Kute Korrespondences, hoping that for each psi-synthetic taken from Earth's soul there is a molecule, secular, more or less ordinary and named, over here—kicking endlessly among the plastic trivia, finding in each Deeper Significance and trying to string them all together like terms of a power series hoping to zero in on the tremendous and secret Function whose name, like the permuted names of God, cannot be spoken [. . .] but to bring them together, in their slick persistence and our preterition . . . to make sense out of it, to find the meanest sharp sliver of truth in so much replication, so much waste. . . . [GR 590]

But as this preterite, we are not, as in the Calvinist dichotomy, without hope or function, just as the present, apocalyptic as it may seem, will not be without a future—even if it is on the other side of an interface.

Enzian, wading through the woods, marshes, and ruins of the Zone, never gives up hope for the future; he thinks, "Somewhere among the wastes of the World, is the key that will bring us back, restore us to our Earth and to our freedom" (*GR* 525). Freedom here is not freedom from the laws of nature, but may mean, for instance, freedom in the Weberian sense of freedom from the oppression of systems (such as Theirs) that are not essential outcomes of the activities of universal principles. For Slothrop, however, freedom is spiritual. As Buber puts it:

The belief in doom is a delusion from the start. The scheme of running down is appropriate only for ordering [the It-world], the severed world-event, objecthood as history. The presence of the [Thou], that which is born of association, is not accessible to this approach, which does not know the actuality of spirit, and this scheme is not valid for the spirit.

Furthermore, Buber goes on to say that whoever (like Pointsman)

is overpowered by the It-world must consider the dogma of an ineluctable running down as a truth that creates a clearing in the jungle. In truth, this dogma only leads him deeper into the slavery of the It-world. But the world of the [Thou] is not locked up. Whoever proceeds toward it, concentrating his whole being, . . . beholds his freedom. And to gain freedom from the belief in unfreedom is to gain freedom.[28]

The second part of Buber's statement describes Slothrop's path. Slothrop, drifting among the human debris of the Zone, does recover his harmonica, his chances for harmony, which had been lost earlier amongst the human wastes of the toilet, and "Slothrop, just suckin' on his harp, is closer to being a spiritual medium than he's been yet, and he doesn't even know it" (*GR* 622). The conscious revelation of what Slothrop still doesn't know is Pynchon's final question to us. Throughout the novel the reader wonders what They know that the preterite—and the reader—do not. If there is any sort of comprehensive answer, it is not to be found within any single metaphorical system. Any such consideration must center around concepts of circularity and transcendence, but there are crucial distinctions between types of circularity and between renewed life and "death transfigured." It is suggested a number of times in the novel that They have perverted the cycle of life for Their own ends. In Kekulé's dream, for instance, Their System steals vital energy from the rest of the world to increase Their own power. The narrator compares living within this system to "riding across the country in a bus driven by a maniac bent on suicide" (*GR* 412). The driver

is waiting beside the door of the bus in his pressed uniform, Lord of the Night he is checking your tickets, your ID and travel papers, and it's the wands of enterprise that dominate tonight ... as he nods you by, you catch a glimpse of his face, his insane, committed eyes, and you remember then, for a terrible few heartbeats, that of course it will end for you all in blood, in shock, without dignity—but there is meanwhile this trip to be on ... over your own seat, where there ought to be an advertising plaque, is instead a quote from Rilke: "Once, only once...." One of Their favorite slogans. No return, no salvation, no Cycle—that's not what They, nor Their brilliant employee Kekulé, have taken the Serpent to mean. No: what the Serpent means is—how's this—that the six carbon atoms of benzene are in fact curled around in a closed ring, *just like that snake with its tail in its mouth,* GET IT? [*GR* 413]

The narrator may interpret this archetypal mythological image as a symbol of a world devouring itself and of the new serpent in a worn Eden, but he is conscious of how any of these interpretations may be misinterpretations that serve Their ends.

Every one of the distinctions represented by each of the metaphors extrapolated in this chapter must be kept in mind in order to preserve the totality of Pynchon's message. If the reader oversimplifies the possibilities of life presented in the novel, he will not be able to appreciate, for instance, precisely what Blicero means in his desire to "break out of this cycle of infection and death" (*GR* 724). To get only part of the point with Pynchon is often to miss the whole point. Again, *Gravity's Rainbow* is "not a disentanglement from, but a progressive *knotting into*" (*GR* 3) the profusion of life seen in all of its potentialities.

5

PARODY AND PARANOIA THROUGH NARRATIVE STRUCTURE

Early critical response to *Gravity's Rainbow* indicated that it was a brilliant but fitful, haphazardly structured novel. The novel's conjunction of slapstick with profundity, and of the narratives of Slothrop, Enzian, and other Rocket Questors with fragments of apparently unrelated fantasy, presents a confusing topography to the reader. Paul Kammerer's concept of seriality, a force which acts selectively on form and function to bring similar configurations together in space and time, provides an apt metaphor for the structure of *Gravity's Rainbow*. Slade and others maintain that Slothrop slips into anti-paranoia in the last quarter of the novel, and that the narrative itself begins to "dissolve" in a like manner. However, anti-paranoia, the state in which "nothing is connected to anything" (*GR* 434), does not adequately describe either Slothrop's condition or the associational relationships of the novel's parts to its other parts and to the whole of theme and plot. Every incident in the novel is connected by form and function to the narrative as a whole.

Perhaps the sections of the novel are connected by filmlike sprocket holes in order to suggest the nature of film narrative, which is often discontinuous in time and space.[1] As Slade points out, film scenes are "obviously" contingent upon but not necessarily linked by cause and effect.[2] Film structure also suggests certain restrictive implications of film narrative, such as the viewer's limited ability to perceive reality through this type of structure. We believe that we are viewing a continuous reality, while actually we perceive an illusion created by the "rapid flashing of successive stills" in an editorially controlled frame and perspective.

There is an obvious associational correspondence as well as a regularity of sequence that unifies the different sections of the novel's narrative, but none of these correspondences is the inevitable end product of character and plot. The narrative structure of *Gravity's Rainbow* recapitulates Mexico's theories of randomness, which determine the parameters of possibility without predicting specific, isolated events. For instance, the reader does not especially need to hear the story of the Floundering Four; it is in no way essential to completing plot, theme, or characterization, but it does help to clarify all three, as well as the narrator's relationship to all three, by parodying certain elements of Slothrop's character and by suggesting his father as one more image of the opposing forces. Furthermore, the element of parody itself constitutes a modification of the way that the narrator—and the reader—perceive Slothrop's quest. In many respects his quest is comic-book fiction, a spectacular contrivance of the narrator that, after all, may not be a complete and faithful representation of the way the narrator views "the assembly of our time."

PARANOIA AND STRUCTURE

I explained in the first chapter that the plot and themes of *Gravity's Rainbow* evolve from the narrator's struggle to comprehend the contemporary world from both individual and societal perspectives. His main problem, both in telling his story and in comprehending the world, is to discover the correct rules of connectedness with which to make sense of things without misrepresenting them. In both fiction-making and life in general, some sense of structure must be imposed on reality in order for human minds to grasp experience and to respond to it. However, because the structures that we select, in either case, must necessarily be based on relatively unproven preconceptions about the world, we are constantly in danger of distorting experience and misunderstanding that world. Therefore, we must be able to structure our perceptions of the world and at the same time be aware of the relatively uncertain value of the structure as an interpretive system. "Creative Paranoia" is the term the characters of the Counterforce employ when playing Their game of controlling the structures through which we perceive reality by creating a We-system. As Roger Mexico and Pirate Prentice observe, the danger of playing Their game, of defining as real and necessary something that may be imaginary or arbitrary, must be weighed against the alternative danger, that we are already in control of our own fate but refuse to recognize our responsibility. (This second danger is of some importance in *The Crying of Lot 49*, where many characters refuse to act because they believe that action is hopeless.) In *Gravity's Rainbow* the narrator castigates Slothrop as one of the "glozing neuters of the world" (*GR* 677), but he also feels sorry for Slothrop's inability to act because he himself feels that the possibilities for action are at least ambiguous: the neuters "have no easy road to haul down, Wear-the-Pantsers, just cause you can't see it doesn't mean it's not there!" (*GR* 677).

The narrator is, of course, the supreme creative paranoid of *Gravity's Rainbow*, for he projects the various hostile They-systems and also suggests the countering We-systems. The paranoia-producing effects of the fictional drug "oneirine theophosphate" parallel certain aspects of the novel's narrative structure. An Oneiromancer is one who claims to divine the future through dreams, and Pynchon translates "theophosphate" for us as "indicating the Presence of God" (*GR* 702). In the hallucinations caused by the drug, "certain themes, 'mantic archetypes' . . . , will find certain individuals again and again" (*GR* 702).

Because analogies with the ghost-life exist, this recurrence phenomenon is known, in the jargon, as "haunting." Whereas other sorts of hallucinations tend to flow by, related in deep ways that aren't accessible to the casual dopefiend, these Oneirine hauntings show a definite narrative continuity, as clearly as, say, the average *Reader's Digest* article. Often they are so ordinary, so conventional—Jeaach calls them "the dullest hallucinations known to psychopharmacology"—that they are only recognized as hauntings through some radical though plausible violation of possibility: the presence of the dead, journeys by the same route and means where one person will set out later but arrive earlier, a printed diagram which no amount of light will make readable. [. . .]
About the paranoia often noted under the drug, there is nothing remarkable. Like other sorts of paranoia, it is nothing less than the onset, the leading edge, of the discovery that *everything is connected*, everything in the Creation, a secondary illumination—not yet blindingly One, but at least connected, and perhaps a route In for those like Tchitcherine who are held at the edge. . . . [*GR* 702-3]

The narrator, as has been noted, counts himself as preterite, and has no other illumination beyond the paranoiac structure of his novel. The section of the novel that directly follows the material just quoted is titled "Tchitcherine's Haunting," but describes an actual event that Tchitcherine has long feared, his apprehension by the Commissariat for Intelligence Activities: "the radical-though-plausible-violation-of-reality" does not occur (*GR* 704). *Gravity's Rainbow* is itself the narrator's haunting by "mantic archetypes" (archetypes that bring on a state of divination); however, the narrator's paranoia is Tchitcherine's reality, and that paranoia becomes the oppressive force that crushes many of the characters. For this reason, the fates of the characters often represent an essentially paranoid vision of their potentialities.

The narrator is also subject to anti-paranoia, "where nothing is connected to anything, a condition not many of us can bear for long" (*GR* 434). As I explained earlier, an optimistic interpretation of the anti-paranoiac state might parallel what Buber describes as a transcendence into an I-Thou state of being: "The relation to the Thou is unmediated. Nothing conceptual intervenes between I and [Thou], no prior knowledge and no imagination; and memory itself is changed as it plunges from practicality into wholeness."[3] Anti-paranoia, like the I-Thou relationship, is impossible to sustain for long; as human beings we must deal with the world of It, of connectedness, the only condition in which we may manipulate our environment. Slothrop achieves an approximation of a continual I-Thou wholeness by giving up his ego and his physical ability to manipulate reality. As Slothrop disintegrates, his temporal bandwidth narrows and he becomes a creature of pure present, for whom time-as-durational-structure no longer exists. Buber says that the I-Thou relationship provides the only true present, the I-It relationship only a past. Buber's words are often an apt description of Slothrop's journey: "Spirit appears in time as a product, even a by-product of nature, and yet it is spirit that envelops nature timelessly."[4]

Paranoia itself is merely a "secondary illumination" that does not actually perceive the real unity of the universe, but is "perhaps a route In for those like Tchitcherine [and Slothrop] who are held at the edge" of true awareness. Slothrop's disintegration is not strictly defined by anti-paranoia, because the "grace" he achieves in abandoning his ego and the world of It involves an intuitive grasp of the real, or perhaps "a real," connectedness of all things that parallels, in some ways, his earlier paranoia:

He used to pick and shovel at the spring roads of Berkshire, April afternoons he's lost, [. . .] days when in superstition and fright he could *make it all fit*, seeing clearly in each an entry in a record, a history: his own, his winter's, his country's . . . instructing him, dunce and drifter, in ways deeper than he can explain, have been faces of children out the train windows, two bars of dance music somewhere, [. . .] laughter out of a cornfield in the early morning [. . .] and now, in the Zone, later in the day he became a crossroad, after a heavy rain he doesn't recall, Slothrop sees a very thick rainbow here, a stout rainbow cock driven down out of the pubic clouds into Earth, green wet valleyed Earth, and his chest fills and he stands crying, not a thing in his head, just feeling natural. . . . [*GR* 626)

Buber maintains that entering into the I-Thou relationship requires both work and "grace," and he says that "relation is reciprocity. My [Thou] acts on me as I act on it. Our students teach us, our works form us. The 'wicked' become a revelation when they are touched by the sacred basic word. How we are educated by children, by animals! Inscrutably involved, we live in the currents of universal reciprocity."[5]

If the structure of the last quarter of the novel does in fact parallel Slothrop's disintegration, we then can expect it to provide an intuitive apprehension of the connectedness of things; we can expect to be instructed by the faces of children and by music half-heard in the distance. However, Slothrop is merely one projected aspect of the narrator, and while the narrator may mean to suggest Slothrop's intuitive grasp of things, he is himself preterite and ego-bound, and the novel proceeds essentially by passages that are symbolic and analytical. Like the Old Doper Dad talking to his Screwed-In Son in "Heart-to-Heart, Man-to-Man," he cannot tolerate the idea of a "one-way trip" into Infinity—he will not trust himself to fate as Enzian and Blicero do but is always rushing back to the touchstones of old "Realityland" (*GR* 698-99).

THE CHAPTERS AS NARRATIVE STRUCTURE

The novel's chapter titles consistently allude to the metaphysical concerns of each section. "Beyond the Zero," which essentially establishes the main themes of the novel as an attempt to understand what occurs beyond the interface of death and to assess the importance of this for our world, has already been discussed. The events of this section include most of the theoretical discussions between Pointsman and Mexico that describe the various scientific conceptions of the nature of connectedness in the universe, the importance of predictability to maintaining the possibilities for free action, the possibility of love as a redeeming force, the improbability of salvation (in the Christmas ruminations of various characters), the fear of annihilation, and the dialectical potentialities of the rocket. The chapter ends with the prophetic revelations of the spirit of Walter Rathenau discoursing on the nature of connectedness.

"Un Perm' au Casino Hermann Goering" suggests the gambling-like laws of randomness that govern events in an apparently perverse world, the discovery of which helps to trigger Slothrop's paranoia. In learning about the construction of the rocket, Slothrop also learns about man's relatedness to the physical laws of the universe and to his own technology. In attempting both to flee from and to discover his fate, Slothrop loses the two closest friends he is to have, Katje and Tantivy, establishing a pattern of isolation that grows throughout the novel.

The epigraph to the third section, "In the Zone," is "Toto, I have a feeling we're not in Kansas any more . . . ," and this chapter suggests a combination of the distorted allegorical normality of Oz with the soul-searching moral angst of Conrad's *Heart of Darkness:* "It's like going to that Darkest Africa to study the natives there, and finding their quaint superstitions taking you over" (*GR* 281). This chapter describes Slothrop's schlepping and scuffling across the Zone, which, in its postwar chaos, is apparently still beyond Their control. The ethnology of the Hereros is given, stressing both their previous psychic unity and their "infection" by "the Christian sickness" (*GR* 320) that creates cultural and psychological fragmentation by preaching antithetical good and evil parts of nature. Tchitcherine is introduced as an apparent Russian counterpart to Slothrop; they not only look somewhat alike and have similar propensities, but even exchange clothing and identities at times. The chaos of the Zone which attends the death of the old culture and the birth of the new, destroys the mind's ability to maintain I-It relationships because it negates all previously accepted structures, and Slothrop's paranoia and his dedication to his quest immediately begin to erode under the influence of "mindless pleasures." As early as Slothrop's departure from Geli, the narrator notes, "It is taking him longer, the longer he's in the Zone, to remember to say *aw quit being a sap.* What is this place doing to his brain?" (*GR* 333). In the *Anubis* episode, which epitomizes the decadent aspects of the dying culture, the narrator more fully describes the effects of the Zone on Slothrop:

Even a month ago, given a day or two of peace, he might have found his way back to the September afternoon, to the stiff cock in his pants sprung fine as a dowser's wand trying to point up at what was hanging there in the sky for everybody. . . .
But nowadays, some kind of space he cannot go against has opened behind Slothrop, bridges that might have led back are down now for good. He is growing less anxious about betraying those who trust him. He feels obligations less immediately. There is, in fact, a general loss of emotion, a numbness he ought to be alarmed at, but can't quite. . . .
[*GR* 490–91]

As Slothrop's connections to the historical forces implied in his quest dissolve after the death of Bianca, the narrator increasingly notes Slothrop's "preterition," another double-edged condition that may mean either the absence of salvation, as in the Calvinist sense, or the Herero word "Mba-kayere," which indicates those "passed over" by von Trotha's search-and-destroy missions in South Africa. If we measure Slothrop's salvation on the worldly scales of Calvinism, he indeed becomes a preterite failure. If, on the other hand, we compare him to those who survived von Trotha, he is a preterite success who has "learned to stand outside of history and watch it, without feeling too much. A little schizoid" (*GR* 362). In this form of preterition, the narrator tells us, Enzian offers Slothrop "a way out" (*GR* 360).

In this section of the novel Slothrop encounters the deathly corruption of pre-World War II Europe on board the *Anubis* (named after the Egyptian god who led the dead to judgment) and the Holy Center of the Rocket in Peenemünde; the latter is both ominous in its charred memories of the rocket and positive in its reaffirmation of life:

"When we came we only cleared out what we needed," Närrisch recalls. "Most of it stayed—the forest, the life . . . there are probably still deer up in there someplace. Big fellows with dark antlers. And the birds— snipes, coots, wild geese—the noise from the testing drove them out to sea, but they'd always come back in when it was quiet again." [*GR* 506]

This section of the novel abounds with ambiguous and contradictory conceptions of the world: Jamf's Nazi chemistry, which preaches the supremacy of the inorganic, is opposed by Lyle Bland's "Masonic" vision of the living earth; the narrator's paranoid history of the Masons is opposed by Slothrop's "transferring to freedom" at Putzi's (*GR* 603), escaping the control of Pointsman's castrating agents; Tchitcherine blossoms into full paranoia, believing in an international rocket cartel plot, but the reader knows that the events that convince him, such as the escape of the Schwarzkommando from his Russian-American ambush, have been haphazardly triggered by Slothrop (*GR* 611). (Later Byron the Bulb suggests that the same events that seem to comprise the paranoid conspiracy are actually "a declaration of brotherhood" between different forms of organic and inorganic life [*GR* 745].)

The unconventional "serial" structure of the fourth chapter of the novel tends to overwhelm readers who are still demanding cause-and-effect progressions. It bears the appropriate epigraph from Richard M. Nixon: "What?" Because it is entitled "The Counterforce," the chapter proceeds in the manner of the Counterforce who "piss on Their rational arrange- ments" (*GR* 639). It is not as difficult to show the connectedness of the events of "The Counterforce" chapter to the themes of the novel as it is to explain the nature of their connectedness to the plot—but only if we consider the plot of the novel to be the story of Slothrop rather than the story of the narrator manipulating the story of Slothrop in an attempt to understand his own world. The plot's frequently random and irrational episodes, such as "The Occupation of Mingeborough," obviously occur in Slothrop's mind as he is disintegrating and serve to connect us to that element of the plot, while others, such as "The Komical Kamikazes," seem to belong only to the narrator, who is watching postwar American television, or engaging in some other activity not available to Slothrop. While the former type of events continues to bring us Slothrop's narrative progress as he disintegrates, the latter type reveals the narrator's reflections on various aspects of the narrative he is constructing. I have already suggested possible explanations for "Byron the Bulb," the "Floundering Four," and most of the other oddities that show up in this part of the novel. A close look at "A Moment of Fun with Takeshi and Ichizo, the Komical Kamikazes" (*GR* 690–92) will clarify both the thematic purposes of this incident and its relationship to the plot of the novel.

Essentially, this comical look at the Kamikazes, men who fulfill their destinies through death, can be seen as a parody of Blicero and Enzian. The fact that the narrator does not wholly believe in the reality of either main character's "mission" must never be lost sight of. Like Enzian and Blicero, Takeshi and Ichizo are a "Mutt and Jeff" pair. Takeshi flies a Zero, perhaps suggesting that his death will not take him "Beyond the Zero" to transcendence. Ichizo flies "a long bomb, actually, with a cockpit for Ichizo to sit in, stub wings, rocket propulsion," similar to the V-2 that Gottfried, and perhaps Enzian, fly to their deaths. However, both Kamikazes are unable to die, to achieve their destinies; each morning they are told "No dying today! So Solly." Instead of killing themselves the two pilots give themselves over to the "mindless pleasures," such as painting themselves blue (Enzian's color) and running around the beach. At the end of this episode, as at the end of the novel itself, the paranoid reader-viewer realizes that he is, in fact, watching a movie rather than reality; in still a second twist, he is not released from this vision but is assured that he will be thrust into its worst conditions, those not included in this World War II situation comedy version of events (*GR* 692). The "Paranoid for the Day" who achieves this "Mystery Insight" is sent on a "one-way trip for one, to the movie's actual location," just as the reader-viewer at the end of the novel is assured that he has "always been at the movies" (*GR* 760), but that, as the movie depicts death, so it is "just at this dark and silent frame, that the pointed tip of the Rocket, falling nearly a mile per second, absolutely and forever without sound, reaches its last unmeasurable gap above the roof of this old theatre, the last delta-t" (*GR* 760). Although the artist is forever locked in the tower of his senses manufacturing his fictional constructions of reality, we all must realize that our own realities are just such constructions, that our lives too are "all theater," and that all these realities may coincide at any moment.

There are discrepancies between levels of reality in this fiction (Takeshi is fat, Enzian is not), just as, the narrator reminds us, there are discrepancies between his fictional reality and the conception of reality that each of us constructs for himself. However, an awareness of the fictional nature of the narrator's (or of Pynchon's) construction will merely alert the true paranoid to how much worse than this things might really be:

You'll while your nights away chasing vampire mosquitoes away from your *own throat!* Getting blind *lost,* out in the middle of torrential tropical downpours! Scooping rat turds out of the enlisted men's water barrel. But it won't be all nighttime giddiness and excitement, Captain, because daytimes, up at five a.m. sharp, you'll be out making the acquaintance of the Kamikaze *Zero* you'll be flying! getting all checked out on those *controls,* making sure you know *just where* that bomb-safety-release is! A-ha-hand of *course,* trying to stay out of the way, of those two *Nonsensical Nips,* Takeshi and Ichizo! as they go about their uproarious weekly adventures, seemingly oblivious to your presence, and the frankly ominous implications of your day's routine. . . . [*GR* 692]

The Komical Kamikazes are, therefore, both a qualification of certain elements of the plot, an anti-paranoid version of Enzian and Blicero, as well as an extension of the paranoid implications of the plot and themes. The fictional process itself poses a threat to the integrity of Creative Paranoia in *Gravity's Rainbow.* The narrator, unlike the Counterforce, is in complete control of the fates of his characters and is in danger of falling into the trap of believing in both his We-system and his They-system as unalterable realities. This results in the apparent discrepancies between the more optimistic vision suggested by an analysis of the novel's metaphorical structures and the more pessimistic vision suggested by an analysis of the plot structure.

This paradox occurs despite the fact that the plot structure of the novel corresponds directly to its thematic content; the plot moves from a more or less logical exposition of the social and psychological problems to be considered, to speculation on the laws of connectedness that govern the universe, to a study of these laws in operation in "the openness of the German Zone" where "hope—and danger—are limitless" (*GR* 265), to an examination of the various possibilities for action given the situation presented in these previous chapters.

The fourth chapter, "The Counterforce," describes four possible alternatives for action, all of which have been discussed to the extent that they are represented by the major metaphorical systems of the novel. The first is Slothrop's separate, personal peace, similar to Rilke's notion of transcendence. The second is the hope for singularities, for dramatic reversals due to unexpected inputs, as represented in the parable of Byron the

Bulb, who continues the quest that Slothrop abandons, and in the strategies of the Counterforce, who hope to reverse Their control. The third is the ritual launching of the 00001 by Enzian and the Schwarzkommandos that may trigger the inception of a new culture. And the fourth is the possible "magic" of love that can give life meaning despite the imminence of death.

CHARACTER AS STRUCTURE

Because the characters of *Gravity's Rainbow* are representations of various important aspects of the narrator, the spectrum of characters provides a structure for all of the major alternatives for the lives of individuals in our age. Throughout the novel the narrator ties the fate of his characters to the fate of western civilization by describing them in relation to their ancestral heritages and then compounding these relationships with non-historical (and noncausal) associations linked to other elements in the plot. For instance, the conjunction of Slothrop, who comes from New England Puritan stock, and Katje, one of whose Calvinist ancestors participated in the extermination of the dodo birds of Mauritius, allows Pynchon to extend his cultural history rather dramatically to include all of the five-hundred-year genocidal reign of Protestantism in Europe and America. At the same time, the narrator presents the story of William Slothrop's Puritan heresy that parallels several of the novel's themes:

> Of course he took it as a parable—knew that the squealing bloody horror at the end of the pike was in exact balance to all their happy sounds, their untroubled pink eyelashes and kind eyes, their smiles, their grace in cross-country movement. It was a little early for Isaac Newton, but feelings about action and reaction were in the air. William must have been waiting for the one pig that wouldn't die, that would validate all the other ones who'd had to, all his Gadarene swine who'd rushed into extinction like lemmings, possessed not by demons but by trust for men, which the men kept betraying . . . possessed by innocence that couldn't lose . . . by faith in William as another variety of pig, at home with the Earth, sharing the same gift of life. . . .
> He wrote a long tract about it presently, called *On Preterition*. It had to be published in England, and is among the first books to've been not only banned but also ceremonially burned in Boston. Nobody wanted to hear about all the Preterite, the many God passes over when he chooses a few for salvation. William argued holiness for these "second Sheep," without whom there'd be no elect. [*GR* 555]

This heresy, the narrator suggests, "could have been the fork in the road America never took, the singular point she jumped the wrong way from....

Might there have been fewer crimes in the name of Jesus, and more mercy in the name of Judas Iscariot?" (*GR* 556). Pigs abound in the next hundred pages of the novel, reinforcing themes serially. Slothrop adopts the role of Plechazunga, the pig-hero who routed a Viking invasion by "appearing suddenly out of a thunderbolt and chasing a score of screaming Norsemen back into the sea" (*GR* 567). Pig Bodine emerges as one of Slothrop's truest friends. Pökler's pig Frieda leads Slothrop to the German rocket scientist, who is leading a reflective hermit's life similar to Slothrop's. Ultimately, by leaping back and forth in history, and by continually foreshadowing the present in his representation of World War II Europe, Pynchon creates a watershed of cultural history in which past, present, and future, science, history, and myth become associated. Plechazunga and Rocketman, Africans and Puritans, Einstein and King Kong join hands, one would imagine, in an organic chain that spins faster and faster until only an elliptical rainbow blur of color is visible. Yet when we examine the fate of the characters, we examine, in effect, the potential of our civilization.

Slothrop's fate has been examined throughout this study; I have traced him from an American naif to a fragmented spirit who stands outside of history and culture. By playing the patterns, "by riding each branch the proper distance, knowing when to transfer, keeping some state of minimum grace though it might often look like he's headed the wrong way," Slothrop finds that "this network of all plots may yet carry him to freedom. He understands that he should not be so paranoid of either Bodine or Solange, but ride instead their kind underground awhile, see where it takes him . . ." (*GR* 603). Slothrop's transcendence is neither pleasurable nor constantly painful, but like the transcendence Rilke spoke of, is of "the emotion that almost startles when happiness falls." Tchitcherine, who I have suggested is an alternate version of Slothrop, only more material (he is made partly of metal) and earthbound, does not transcend but descends, Tannhäuserwise, into pantheistic creation (*GR* 720) and love (*GR* 734); Geli alone will remain in his world, and so, like Slothrop, he is lost to history.

At the opposite extreme from the personal peace pursued by Tchitcherine and Slothrop is the transcendence of Enzian and Blicero. Blicero is positive of the cyclicality of the universe, but he believes that the natural cycles have been perverted by the European "order of Analysis and Death" (*GR* 722) that prevents transcendence into spiritual wholeness. Blicero tells Gottfried, whom he is soon to launch northward in the 00000: "I want to break out—to leave this cycle of infection and death. I want to be taken in love: so taken that you and I, and death, and life, will be gathered, inseparable, into the radiance of what we would become" (*GR* 724).

Enzian, like Blicero, is searching for a return to unity and rebirth:

His tribe believed long ago that each sunset is a battle. In the north, where the sun sets, live the one-armed warriors, the one-legged and one-eyed, who fight the sun each evening, who spear it to death until its blood runs out over the horizon and sky. But under the earth, in the night, the sun is born again, to come back each dawn, new and the same. But we, Zone-Hereros, under the earth, how long will we wait in this north, this locus of death? Is it to be reborn? or have we really been buried for the last time, buried facing north like the rest of our dead, and like all the holy cattle ever sacrificed to the ancestors? North is death's region. There may be no gods, but there is a pattern: names by themselves may have no magic, but the *act* of naming, the physical utterance, obeys the pattern. Nordhausen means dwelling in the north. The Rocket had to be produced out of a place called Nordhausen. The town adjoining was named Bleicheröde as a validation, a bit of redundancy so that the message would not be lost. The history of the old Hereros is one of lost messages. It began in mythical times, when the sly hare who nests in the Moon brought death among men, instead of the Moon's true message. The true message has never come. Perhaps the Rocket is meant to take us there someday, and then the Moon will tell us its truth at last. There are those down in the Erdschweinhöhle, younger ones who've only known white autumn-prone Europe, who believe Moon is their destiny. But older ones can remember that Moon, like Ndjambi Karunga, is both the bringer of evil and its avenger. . . . [*GR* 322]

The warriors of the myth, who are physically fragmented, sound much like Blicero's infected Europeans, who have divided the world into antitheses through their analysis. Blicero has a vision of the Moon as "Death's Kingdom," in which the Moon's true message, which he supposes to be one of transcendence, has been perverted by Their synthesis and control into a living death where "men have a frosty appearance, hardly solid, no more alive than memories, . . . year after hoarfrost year out in the white latitudes, in empty colony" (*GR* 723). Blicero wishes he "could recover it all. Those men had once been through a tragic day—ascent, fire, failure, blood" (*GR* 723). He seems to be the spiritual opposite of Rathenau, who does not believe in the movement from "death to any rebirth," but only from "death to death-transfigured" (*GR* 166), another possible permutation of death and of transcendence noted by the narrator.

Enzian, unlike his counterpart Blicero, is not so certain that unity cannot be recovered. He searches among the wastes of the world for "the key that will bring us back, restore us to our Earth and to our freedom" (*GR* 525). Blicero is a charismatic figure, a singular agent of destiny fulfilling a personal fate. As Enzian says: "Whatever happened at the end, he has transcended. Even if he's only dead. He's gone beyond *his* pain, *his* sin—driven deep into Their province" (*GR* 660-61). Enzian, on the other hand, has not transcended but has remained within the realm of history to lead his people. As a leader he has gained perspective at the expense of personal involvement and has become an "estranged figure at a certain elevation and distance . . . who has lost everything else but this vantage. There is . . . no human heart left in which I exist" (*GR* 660). His mission may be suicidal, not, as many critics have indicated, for his entire race, but in the possibility that Enzian himself may, by replacing Gottfried in the 00001, be sacrificing himself to rejuvenate his society. (In this sense Enzian seems modeled after Martin Luther King, which explains Pynchon's attributing King's "My people, I have had a vision" speech to Enzian.) He is pitting his people against Their culture, which has been used to frighten humans into submission with lies about death and about Their ability to protect us from death if we behave. The rocket, says Enzian,

"comes as the Revealer. Showing that no society can protect, never could—they are as foolish as shields of paper. [. . .] They have lied to us. They can't keep us from dying, so They lie to us about death. [. . .] Before the Rocket we went on believing, because we wanted to. But the Rocket can penetrate, from the sky, at any given point. Nowhere is safe. We can't believe Them any more. Not if we are still sane, and love the truth." [*GR* 728]

Above all, Enzian wants to restore humanity's sense of harmony with an ambivalent universe by exposing Their lies about death, Paradoxically—to a westerner, though not to a Herero—destruction and death will give man a new lease on life. The narrator exposes Their lies about death and about disgrace, its corollary, in his description of the life in the Zone of the DP child Ludwig, who sustains himself by catering to the sexual perversions of adults: "Ludwig has fallen into a fate worse than death and found it's negotiable. So not all lemmings go over the cliff, and not all children are preserved against snuggling into the sin of profit. To expect anymore, or less, of the Zone is to disagree with the terms of the Creation" (*GR* 729).

Because Enzian's goal is not racial suicide, he forcibly restrains the Empty Ones whose doctrine is the Final Zero (*GR* 525) which offers nothing at all beyond death. Enzian wants to take part in the mythic Herero battle between death and rebirth by firing the 00001 due north to blast open the frozen kingdom that restrains the sun. Therefore, the firing of the 00001 will recapitulate not only Blicero's attempt to "break out—to leave this cycle of infection and death" (*GR* 724) but also the original Herero myth of rebirth from death. The due north firings of Enzian and Blicero complete a circle of firings that fulfill "the logic of the mandalas" (*GR* 707). Mircea Eliade has pointed out that the mandala is primarily an "imago-mundi," a miniature representation of the cosmos of the pantheon, whose construction is equivalent to a magical recreation of the world.[6] In *Gravity's Rainbow* Kabbalist spokesman Steve Edelman recapitulates a similar cosmogonic myth. At the Creation he says:

"God sent out a pulse of energy into the void. It presently branched and sorted into ten distinct spheres or aspects, corresponding to the numbers 1–10 [paralleling the Rocket's countdown]. These are known as the Sephiroth. To return to God, the soul must negotiate each of the Sephiroth, from ten back to one. [. . .]
"Now the Sephiroth fall into a pattern, which is called the Tree of Life. It is also the body of God. [. . .]
"Some Sephiroth are active or masculine, others passive or feminine. But the Tree itself is a unity, rooted exactly at the Bodenplatte. It is the axis of a particular Earth, a new dispensation, brought into being by the Great Firing." [*GR* 753]

Although he meets with representatives of the Counterforce, and one of the Schwarzkommandos serves as a liaison man with them (*GR* 638), Enzian's path is not the same as that of the Counterforce. Its members hope for a political overthrow of Their control (*GR* 539). The Counterforce occupies the middle ground between Slothrop's personal salvation and Enzian's mythological rejuvenation of our culture. The Counterforce is composed of characters who have served Them in one way or another, and the first task of each member is to overcome shame for having aided Them; Pirate and Katje, for instance, are assigned to a special group for Counterforce personnel who have at least figuratively murdered each other in Their service (*GR* 542). As the narrator tells us in his remarks about the Ego (*GR* 712–13), to work in the world is to work in Their World— "No one has ever left the Firm alive" (*GR* 543). The best anyone in the Counterforce can do is to be a "double agent." To succeed in this role one must become "actively at peace," "fully expecting to die" (*GR* 541); it is of course no accident that these phrases describe Leni Pökler's delta-t experience in which the individual loses his personal fear, as well as Buber's state of I-Thou in which the individual plays a double agent between the worlds of Thou and It.

The members of the Counterforce want to recover that which is most important to most of us—a sense of everyday reality that is not debased by Their touch. However, of all the possibilities for action suggested in the novel, this seems the least likely to succeed. The strategies of Bodine and Mexico only seem good for laughs and for buoying their own spirits. Katje has the opposite problem from Slothrop, who dissolves physically; she has a "leukemia of the soul" (*GR* 658) that threatens her spiritual disappearance at moments late in the novel, and that prevents her from "passing into the All":

> Her masochism [Weissmann wrote from the Hague] is reassurance for her. That she can still be hurt, that she is human and can cry at pain. Because, often, she will forget. I can only try to guess how terrible that must be. . . . So, she needs the whip. She raises her ass not in surrender, but in despair—like your fears of impotence, and mine: can it still . . . will it fail. . . . But of true submission, of letting go the self and passing into the All, there is nothing, not with Katje. [*GR* 662]

"Their" life has deadened her to reality, and even as she tries to fight Them she feels herself losing touch with any meaningful sense of reality (*GR* 659).

We learn near the end of the novel that the Counterforce as an organization destroys itself in the late 1960s, perhaps through its own diversity or its innate corruption—its tendency as an institution to rationalize (*GR* 738-39). This is one of the narrator's most pessimistic notes, and he tries to counter it to some extent with Roger Mexico's bravura promises to fight on to the death. The name "Mexico" seems to suggest certain similarities with the Counterforce to Pynchon, who, it is rumored, often lives in that country; Mexico has been "colonized" and infected by the United States but has managed to retain some sense of integrity and is still open to more radical social and political change than is the United States. From the beginning of the novel Mexico is engaged in creating a meaningful life for himself. While Slothrop continually abandons his chances for love in his fear of death and control, Roger faces death squarely in his affair with Jessica. The narrator sees Mexico's love as another way of confronting death by living in the moment, as Leni Pökler does:

> His life had been tied to the past. He'd seen himself a point on a moving wavefront, propagating through sterile history—a known past, a projectable future. But Jessica was the breaking of the wave. Suddenly there was a beach, the unpredictable . . . new life. Past and future stopped at the beach: that was how he'd set it out. But he wanted to believe it too, the same way he loved her, past all words—believe that no matter how bad the time, nothing was fixed, everything could be changed and she could always deny the dark sea at his back, love it away. And (selfishly) that from a somber youth, squarely founded on Death—along for Death's

ride—he might, with her, find his way to love and to joy. He'd never told her, he avoided telling himself, but that was the measure of his faith, as this seventh Christmas of the War came wheeling in another charge at his skinny, shivering flank. . . . [*GR* 126]

Mexico's analogy of his love to a new sense of the present completely separable in quality from the past and future once again recalls Buber, and Leni's delta-t. That Mexico loses Jessica at the end of the novel is of course a qualification of this strategy, but between the zero of annihilation and the one of transcendence Mexico finds ground to hope that he might "find his way to life and to joy." Love commutes the sentence of death by denying its ability to negate everything else meaningful to the individual. Tchitcherine, who has always wanted to murder his brother for causing his communist-style preterition (*GR* 705), is "blinded" by Geli's love and passes his brother by in the night: "This is magic. Sure—but not necessarily fantasy. Certainly not the first time a man has passed his brother by, at the edge of the evening, often forever, without knowing it" (*GR* 735).

As Bodine suggests, "right reason" will not defeat Them and Their death, but grace, "the physical grace to keep it working," might (*GR* 741). Unfortunately, it seems far easier for most of us to believe in right reason than in grace, and the narrator would argue that this is precisely Their strength. But the possibility of cultural resurrection through Enzian's strategy and the possibility of achieving a state of grace through love are certainly no less real than Slothrop's erections or these paranoid divinations of the narrator. To accept the possibility that Slothrop might be "in love, in sexual love, with his, and his race's, death" (*GR* 738), is also to accept the possibility that "somewhere, among the wastes of the World, is the key that will bring us back, restore us to our Earth and to our freedom" (*GR* 525). As Mexico thinks of his love for Jessica, "In a life he has cursed, again and again, for its need to believe in the transobservable, here is the first, the very first real magic: data he can't argue away" (*GR* 38).

PATTERN AND MEANING IN *GRAVITY'S RAINBOW*

An "objective" reading of *Gravity's Rainbow* is difficult to attain because the reader will become emotionally involved in one vision or another, caught up indiscriminately in paranoias of annihilation or transcendence. The plot structure of the novel promises connectedness and symmetry; because characters meet their destinies, the novel mirrors the end of each of our lives, the "last delta-t," an "immeasurable gap" away (*GR* 760). The universe, on the other hand, seems to promise some kind of continuity—if They haven't rerouted it. (The paranoids have no easy road to haul down, Wear-the-Pantsers, just cause you can't see it doesn't mean it's not there.) At the same time, those who live simply for the mindless pleasures of the day, escape both the fear of death and the fear of control: "While nobles are crying in their night's chains, the squires sing. The terrible politics of the Grail can never touch them. Song is the magic cape" (*GR* 701). The narrator pretends to be a squire, but he worries too much for the role. But neither does he count himself as a charismatic leader. He is, by his own account, the Fool who fulfills his courtly role as an entertainer and advisor by disguising his meanings as "mindless pleasures."

Gravity's Rainbow delineates the possibilities for the future, but Pynchon finally promises neither annihilation nor transcendence; he is sure only that life as we know it is changing. With creative paranoia Pynchon balances his fears for the future with his hopes. He originally entitled his work *Mindless Pleasures* because it is neither a prophecy of doom nor a call to arms, but a visceral pleasure and a nightmare—a "haunting"—of which we may partake in the time we have left:

The wine will operate on whatever happens. Didn't you wake up to find a knife in your hand, your head down a toilet, the blur of a long sap about to smash your upper lip, and sink back down to the old red and capillaried nap where none of this could possibly be happening? and wake again to a woman screaming, again to the water of the canal freezing your drowned eye and ear, again to too many Fortresses diving down the sky, again, again. . . . But no, never real.

A wine rush: a wine rush is defying gravity, finding yourself on the elevator ceiling as it rockets *upward*, and no way to get down. You separate in two, the basic Two, and each self is aware of the other. [*GR* 743]

The narrator is aware of the risks of inaction, but is driven to it by the confusion he encounters in analyzing contemporary life. His role as court jester allows him to jog the thinking of those in power occasionally, but there seems to be just a tinge of bitterness because of his general impotence and frustration.

Slothrop fails, in the end, to fulfill the role of the picaresque hero who finds a home; thus, *Gravity's Rainbow* departs from the traditional picaresque structure. Neither is the novel structured as allegory, since there is no ultimate victory or defeat, no clear-cut good or evil. The contents of the novel promise to violate any common literary structure, whether largely aesthetic or largely mythic or allegorical. Claude Lévi-Strauss differentiates the procedures of these two extremes in narrative by assuming that the starting point of any work of art is a set of one or more objects and one or more events united by the revelation of a common structure. Myths travel the same road but start with a structure that produces what is itself an object consisting of a set of events. Art, he believes, proceeds from the conjunction of an object and an event to the discovery of its structure, while myth starts from a structure by means of which it constructs and combines an object and an event.[7]

Gravity's Rainbow is aesthetic in that Pynchon has apparently begun with a set, a very large set, of cultural objects and events and has attempted to reveal their common structure. But the structure he is interested in is not primarily aesthetic, concerned with the symmetry of the work itself, but physical, concerned with the nature of the universe outside of the work. Therefore he is involved in creating a myth of our time from the emerging structures of our culture and from apparent physical laws; the narrator conspicuously manipulates his characters so that they fulfill those possible patterns. One may say either that the patterns themselves are not definitively known, and that therefore the ultimate relationship of the objects to each other remains ambiguous, or vice versa. Any attempt to place the structure of *Gravity's Rainbow* in a traditional genre probably will be rendered meaningless by qualifications. This is why I have described it as a Creative Paranoia. Perhaps the most helpful description that we can apply to its structure is Edward Mendelson's invention of the category of "encyclopedic narrative," which gathers examples from the full range of a culture's knowledge and organizes them in a single narrative that displays "the limits and possibilities of action" within a culture. The implication of defining *Gravity's Rainbow* in this manner is that it will somehow tell us something meaningful about the present state of our culture and will indicate, perhaps, something about its future.

6

COSMIC GOSSIP—THE FUTURE

It is rumored that Pynchon's next novel involves research about the Mason-Dixon line; his attention to historical events and cultural crises makes it seem plausible that he will be examining the formation of modern attitudes from the emergence of the United States as an industrial society. *Gravity's Rainbow*, like *V.*, embraced the general aspects of western civilization; perhaps Pynchon's next novel, like *The Crying of Lot 49*, will examine western culture through the focus of America; perhaps it will extrapolate our possibilities for the future, or eulogize our failure as the end product of a thousand years of European cultural development.

Many readers expect fiction to help to create cultural values or to provide role models for us in these confusing times. Robert Penn Warren suggests that one of the primary purposes of art in our society is to provide new models for "regenerate" concepts of self, because our technological society has caused the progressive decay of the individual's sense of self.[1] As we saw in discussing Weber, bureaucratic, industrialized society obliterates the variety of characteristics and values that form the backbone of a democratic culture. According to Warren, the loss of the positive sense of self that occurs when diverse individuality is sacrificed to a "rational" conformity has led in part to modern literature's conceptions of the antihero and to the schlemiel "hero as slob" of the black humorists. Warren says that the literary models of the "torn self may find redemption," but he looks to Oedipus and Lear for examples and then returns to modern fiction for exceptions: Warren sees Clyde Griffiths in *An American Tragedy* affirm the nature and meaning of a self only in the painful story of an individual who lacks the very notion of selfhood; Heller's characters in *Catch-22* and Pynchon's in *V.* are death-dancers in a maniacal world in which automatism has replaced self.

It is easy enough to apply Warren's suggestion that our literature provides a "'model' of self in its adventures of selfhood" to the failed romantic heroes of Fitzgerald and the cynically nihilistic but metaphysically groping and uneasy protagonists of Hemingway, as well as to Pynchon's Oedipa Maas. When placed in the context of American novels that deal with the importance of technology to the individual's concept of self, *Gravity's Rainbow* represents a variety of characters undergoing the adventures of selfhood. Pointsman is seeking to define himself in the terminology of the mechanistic society, and his passion to fit Slothrop into behavioristic definitions of man, or else to destroy him, seems to be partly a result of Pointsman's own need for self-definition. Slothrop fails in his quest for self-definition and disintegrates into selflessness. Again, we see that Mexico is seeking a middle way between Slothrop's totally formless egolessness and the sterile, restrictive, mechanistic definition of self proposed by Pointsman. Mexico accommodates the impact of technology on his conception of his self and his sense of reality by defining the course of society within the "rational" probabilities of his mathematical construction of the universe, and retaining a sense of personal freedom according to the laws of randomness that govern all individual occurrences within the set of probabilities. Mexico, like Pynchon himself, never tries to deny that he is living in a technological society that limits the alternatives for individual self-definition, but he struggles to establish a strong sense of himself within the possible alternatives, even to the extent of fighting against what appears to be the probable failure of his love affair with Jessica.

The importance of technology in Pynchon's novels is readily apparent; the surfaces of these works are all heavily populated with the machinery of our age. Unfortunately, most critical commentary has been confined to remarks about Pynchon's background as an engineering student, his fine grasp of technological systems and their possibilities as metaphor, and a generally oversimplified version of his supposed romantic fear of what technology is doing to mankind. What Pynchon really fears is not technology per se, but the passivity it creates in human beings, the great power it gives to a few who are not passive, and what he describes in *V.* as a tendency toward inanimateness of spirit and the dissipation of all human qualities beyond the purely mechanical and material producing. Although it may be a sign of sad times when an oscilloscope replaces the Young Lady from Kent in our sexual limericks, the real dangers that Pynchon suggests are the degree to which technological advancement has displaced all other human drives and the degree to which our technology alienates us from our personal lives by making every aspect of our industry, economy, and society seem unrelated by any direct connections to us. Pökler does not know his own daughter any more than he knows the importance of the work he does on the 00000.

The goal of any technological system in any form, even film, for instance, is technological efficiency. This requires the complete control of an environment and the abolition of any freedom of choice. This control is one reason why Enzian, Springer, and other characters in *Gravity's Rainbow* are often unclear about the connections between the inanimate technology that controls man in order to increase productivity and an animate, self-serving They who might control man for some other end.

Pynchon is not so naive as to suppose the road to recovery of America lies along a return to pastoralism and a denial of all our technology. Slothrop achieves some element of peace in a pastoral setting—the Zone is virtually a parody of that, a despoiled garden—but his peace is otherworldly and does not mark a reconciliation of pastoral and technological values. Roger Mexico and Jessica experience some of their happiest moments in a deserted cottage in rural Kent, but they are both "children of the war" and of its technology, and Mexico is well aware of his own sentimentality in this idyll. Lyle Bland's reverie on "the living Earth" is not pastoral; he finds that gravity "is really something eerie, Messianic, extrasensory in Earth's mindbody" (*GR* 590). Pynchon suggests that the tensions between man and machine, man and nature, and machine and nature may, in fact, be unnecessary if we understand the true nature of each. Technology is not evil in itself, despite the predominant image of the V-2. Remember, we are dealing with a rocket that may be either for travel to the stars or for our own destruction. The antagonism in *Gravity's Rainbow* is not between the garden and the machine, but between uses of the machine.

The narrator of *Gravity's Rainbow* is a contemporary individual trying to invent, to "assemble" a self with which to confront our world. It is a self constructed from an immense range of cultural, social, and technological roles, reflecting a broad spectrum of environmental influences, which may have to face any one of a variety of possible futures; and in the end, even if it could be perfectly constructed, this self might yet prove inadequate for survival. Indeed, confronted with this kind of task on a day of ill omens, you might well find yourself driven back to the tube to watch a seventh rerun of the Takeshi and Ichizo Show, to light a cigarette and try to forget the whole thing. . . .

Nothing can be guaranteed; gravity provides the only free ride.

For the future, then, Pynchon can recommend only that we keep ourselves open to possibility, that we recognize the parameters of our responsibility to ourselves, and that we don't deny that we must work for freedom and self-realization among those possibilities and within those parameters. T. S. Eliot, investigating the roots of his own life in America and the roots of American life in Europe in *Four Quartets*, parallels many of Pynchon's themes and concerns, and like Pynchon concludes only that

> We shall not cease from exploration
> And the end of all our exploring
> Will be to arrive where we started
> And know the place for the first time.[2]

We can merely hope that Thomas Pynchon will continue to share his explorations with us for some time to come.

NOTES

1: INTRODUCTION

1. "The Most Irresponsible Bastard," p. 24.
2. Among these are Roger Sale, "American Fiction in 1973," and Eric Storris, "The Worldly Palimpest of Thomas Pynchon."
3. Thomas Pynchon, *The Crying of Lot 49*, p. 10.
4. *The Crying of Lot 49*, p. 138.
5. Rainer Maria Rilke, *Duino Elegies*, trans. J. B. Leishman and Stephen Spender (New York: W. W. Norton & Co., 1967), p. 21. This is the same translation Pynchon acknowledges in *Gravity's Rainbow*.
6. "Rainbow Corner."
7. "Rainbow Corner." Mendelson published a fuller analysis of "the encyclopedic narrative" in *MLN* 91 (1976): 1267-75; and in *Mindful Pleasures*, ed. David Leverenz and George Levine.
8. "Pynchon's *The Crying of Lot 49:* The Novel as Subversive Experience."
9. Thomas Pynchon, *Gravity's Rainbow* (New York: Viking Press, 1973). All further references to the novel are to this edition. Because of Pynchon's frequent and unusual use of ellipses, my editorial ellipses are bracketed.
10. Scott Sanders, "Pynchon's Paranoid History," p. 177.
11. Among these are Josephine Hendin, "What Is Thomas Pynchon Telling Us?"; Neil Schmitz, "Describing the Demon: The Appeal of Thomas Pynchon"; and Earl Rovit, "Some Shapes in Recent American Fiction."
12. Pynchon's title for the novel was originally *Mindless Pleasures,* a phrase that will be examined in a later chapter. Reportedly, the title *Gravity's Rainbow* was suggested to Pynchon by his editor at Viking Press, and Pynchon agreed to the change. This does not necessarily minimize the importance of the final title phrase, since the same source also told me that Pynchon oversaw the original publication of the novel with great care and allowed only a few word changes to be made in the new French translation. (Viking Press has been instructed by Pynchon to refuse access to *any* information pertaining to the publication of *Gravity's Rainbow,* and, therefore, these comments, made at the 1975 MLA convention seminar on Pynchon, are probably not verifiable through any official source.)
13. Among these are Melvin Maddocks, "Paleface Takeover"; Joseph Sperry, "Henry Adams and Thomas Pynchon: The Entropic Movements of Self, Society and Truth."

14.   Among these are George Levine, "V-2"; W. T. Lhamon; Lance Ozier; and, in part, Edward Mendelson.

2: NARRATIVE POINT OF VIEW

1.   Tony Tanner, *City of Words: American Fiction 1950-1970*, pp. 15-31.
2.   The sprocket holes were, according to a number of sources, the invention of Viking Press editors.
3.   *V.* (New York: Bantam Books, 1964), p. 51. All subsequent references to *V.* are to this edition.
4.   Quoted by James Earl, "Scientific and Philosophical Themes in *Gravity's Rainbow*," presented at the 1975 MLA convention seminar on Pynchon, p. 10.
5.   Siegfried Kracauer, *From Caligari to Hitler* (Princeton: Princeton Univ. Press, 1947), pp. 61-76.
6.   "*Gravity's Rainbow*," p. 14.
7.   Locke, p. 2.
8.   *The Haunted Screen* (Berkeley: Univ. of California Press, 1969), p. 15.
9.   Kracauer, p. 73; and Arthur Lenning, *The Silent Voice* (self-published, 1969), p. 217.
10.   James is quoted by Richard Chase, *The American Novel and Its Tradition* (Garden City, N. Y.: Doubleday, 1957), p. 25.
11.   "Objective Image and Act of Mind in Modern Poetry," PMLA 91 (January 1976): 104-5.
12.   *V.*, p. 259.
13.   *Tractatus Logico-Philosophicus* (London: Routledge & Kegan Paul, 1961), p. 145.
14.   Angus Fletcher, *Allegory: The Theory of a Symbolic Mode* (Ithaca: Cornell Univ. Press, 1970), p. 301.

3: CHARACTERIZATION AND PERSONAL SALVATION

1.   "World Enough, and Time," p. 61.
2.   "The Enigma Variation of Thomas Pynchon," p. 71.
3.   Forster, *Aspects of the Novel* (New York: Harcourt, Brace & World, Inc., 1955), p. 63.
4.   "Pynchon's Tapestries on the Western Wall," p. 216.
5.   "Pynchon in *Gravity's Rainbow:* Love among the Runes, or, Miltonic in the Gloaming," p. 8.
6.   *The Kid* (Edinburgh, G. B.: John Lehmann, 1947), p. vi.
7.   *A Cheerful Nihilism* (Bloomington: Indiana Univ. Press, 1971), p. 6.
8.   Alfred Douglas, *The Tarot* (Baltimore: Penguin Books, 1972), pp. 48-49.
9.   Cuthbert Hadden, *The Operas of Wagner* (London: T. C. and E. C. Jack, 1908), p. 222.
10.   Douglas, p. 218.
11.   Douglas, p. 193.
12.   Forster, p. 63.
13.   Marjorie Kaufman, "Brünhilde and the Chemists: Women in *Gravity's Rainbow*," in *Mindful Pleasures*, ed. George Levine and David Leverenz, pp. 197-228; Edward Mendelson, "Gravity's Encyclopedia," in *Mindful Pleasures*, pp. 161-196; Joseph Slade, "Escaping Rationalization: Options for the Self in *Gravity's Rainbow*."
14.   Levine, "V-2." p. 525.
15.   Mathew Winston, "The Quest for Pynchon," p. 280.
16.   Forster, pp. 160-61.

17.　Eleanor Bertine, *Jung's Contribution to Our Time* (New York: Putnam's, 1967), p. 3.
18.　Slade, "Escaping Rationalization," p. 29.
19.　Jolande Jacobi, *The Psychology of C. G. Jung* (New Haven: Yale University Press, 1962), pp. 48–49.
20.　Slade, *Thomas Pynchon*, p. 237.

4: SOCIO-CULTURAL METAPHORS

1.　"Some Shapes in Recent American Fiction," p. 553.
2.　"Pynchon's Linguistic Demon: *The Crying of Lot 49*," p. 49.
3.　Henry Adams, *The Education of Henry Adams* (Boston: Houghton Mifflin, 1961), p. 489.
4.　"Entropy in Pynchon's *Crying of Lot 49*," p. 22.
5.　"The Sacred, the Profane, and *The Crying of Lot 49*," in *Individual and Community: Variations on a Theme in American Fiction*, ed. K. Baldwin and D. Kirby, pp. 200–202.
6.　Lance Ozier, "The Calculus of Transformation: More Mathematical Imagery in *Gravity's Rainbow*," p. 200.
7.　Ozier, p. 200.
8.　Martin Buber, *I and Thou*, tr. Walter Kaufman (New York: Charles Scribner's Sons, 1970), p. 148.
9.　Buber, p. 62.
10.　Buber, pp. 101–2.
11.　"Scientific and Philosophical Themes in *Gravity's Rainbow*," presented at the 1975 MLA convention seminar on Pynchon, pp. 4–5.
12.　E. M. Butler, *Rainer Maria Rilke* (New York: The Macmillan Co., 1941), p. 358.
13.　Rainer Maria Rilke, *Duino Elegies*, ed. and tr. J. B. Leishman and Stephen Spender (New York: W. W. Norton & Co., 1967), p. 24. All further quotations refer to this edition. Pynchon acknowledges this edition on the copyright page of *Gravity's Rainbow*.
14.　Rilke, *Elegies*, pp. 9–10.
15.　Rilke, *Elegies*, p. 87.
16.　Rilke, *Elegies*, pp. 87–88.
17.　Rilke, *Elegies*, p. 108.
18.　Rilke, *Elegies*, p. 113.
19.　Joseph Slade, "Escaping Rationalization: Options for the Self in *Gravity's Rainbow*," pp. 29–31.
20.　*Understanding Media: The Extensions of Man* (New York: Signet Classics, 1964), pp. 19–21.
21.　From H. H. Gerth and C. Wright Mills, *Max Weber* (New York: Oxford University Press, 1969), p. 71.
22.　*Gesammelte Aufsaetze zur Religionssoziologie* (Tübingen, J. C. B. Mohr, 1963), 1: 252.
23.　Scott Sanders, "Pynchon's Paranoid History," p. 186.
24.　Sanders, p. 188.
25.　Robert Donington, *Wagner's "Ring" and Its Symbols* (London: Faber & Faber, 1963), p. 21.
26.　*The Quest: History and Meaning in Religion* (Chicago: Univ. of Chicago Press, 1971), p. 126.
27.　Eliade, p. 77.
28.　Buber, p. 107.

5: PARODY AND PARANOIA THROUGH NARRATIVE STRUCTURE

1.   It is rumored that the sprocket holes were the invention of a Viking editor, although this is difficult to verify.
2.   Joseph Slade, *Thomas Pynchon*, p. 220.
3.   Martin Buber, *I and Thou*, tr. Walter Kaufman (New York: Charles Scribner's Sons, 1970), p. 62.
4.   Buber, p. 75.
5.   Buber, p. 67.
6.   *Myth and Reality*, tr. Willard Trask (New York: Harper & Row Publishers, 1963), p. 25.
7.   *The Savage Mind* (Chicago: Univ. of Chicago Press, 1970), p. 26.

6: COSMIC GOSSIP—THE FUTURE

1.   "Democracy and Poetry," *Southern Review* 9, no. 1 (January 1975): 15.
2.   *Four Quartets* (New York: Harcourt, Brace & World, 1943), p. 59.

SELECTED BIBLIOGRAPHY

WORKS BY THOMAS PYNCHON

The Crying of Lot 49. New York: Bantam Books, 1966.
"Entropy." In *Twelve from the Sixties*, edited by Richard Kostelanetz, pp. 22–35. New York: Dell, 1967.
Gravity's Rainbow. New York: Viking Press, 1973.
"A Journey into the Mind of Watts." In *Man against Poverty: World War III*, edited by Arthur Blaustein and Roger Woock, pp. 146–58. New York: Random House, 1968.
"Lowlands." In *New World Writing 16*, pp. 85–108. Philadelphia: J. B. Lippincott, 1960.
"Mortality and Mercy in Vienna." *Epoch* 5 (spring 1959): 195–213.
"The Secret Integration." *Saturday Evening Post*, 19 December 1965, pp. 36–51.
"The Small Rain." *The Cornell Writer*, March 1959.
"Under the Rose." *The Noble Savage* 3 (1961): 223–51.
V. New York: Bantam Books, 1964.

WORKS ABOUT PYNCHON

Abernathy, Peter L. "Entropy in Pynchon's *Crying of Lot 49*." *Critique* 14, no. 2 (1972): 18–33.
Cowart, David. "Pynchon's *The Crying of Lot 49* and the Paintings of Remedios Varo." *Critique* 18, no. 3 (1977): 19–26.
Davis, Robert M. "Parody, Paranoia, and the Dead End of Language in *The Crying of Lot 49*." *Genre* 5 (1972): 367–77.
DeFeo, Ronald, "Fiction Chronicle." *Hudson Review* 26 (winter 1973–74): 773–75.
Earl, James. "Scientific and Philosophical Themes in *Gravity's Rainbow*." Presented at the 1975 MLA convention seminar on Pynchon.
Fahy, Joseph. "Thomas Pynchon's *V.* and Mythology." *Critique* 18, no. 3 (1977): 5–18.
Friedman, Alan, and Manfred Puetz. "Science as Metaphor: Thomas Pynchon and *Gravity's Rainbow*." *Contemporary Literature* 15 (summer 1974): 345–59.
Golden, Robert E. "Mass Man and Modernism: Violence in Pynchon's *V.*" *Critique* 14, no. 2 (1972): 5–17.

130

Greenburg, Alvin. "The Underground Woman: An Excursion into the V-ness of Thomas Pynchon." *Chelsea* 27 (1969): 58–65.

Harris, Charles B. "Thomas Pynchon and the Entropic Vision." In *Contemporary American Novelists of the Absurd.* New Haven: College and University Press, 1971.

Hausdorff, Don. "Thomas Pynchon's Multiple Absurdities." *Contemporary Literature* 7 (1966): 258–69.

Henderson, Harry B. *Versions of the Past: The Historical Imagination in American Fiction.* New York: G. P. Putnam's Sons, 1974.

Hendin, Josephine. "What Is Thomas Pynchon Telling Us?" *Harper's* 250 (March 1975): 82–92.

Henkle, Roger B. "Pynchon in *Gravity's Rainbow:* Love Among the Runes, or, Miltonic in the Gloaming." Presented at the 1975 MLA convention seminar on Pynchon.

———. "Pynchon's Tapestries on the Western Wall." *Modern Fiction Studies* 17, (1971): 207–20.

Hunt, John W. "Comic Escape and Anti-Vision: The Novels of Joseph Heller and Thomas Pynchon." In *Adversity and Grace in Recent American Fiction,* edited by Nathan Scott, pp. 87–112. Chicago: University of Chicago Press, 1968.

Jordan, Clive. "World Enough, and Time." *Encounter* 42 (February 1974): 61–65.

Kaufman, Marjorie. "Brünnhilde and the Chemists: Women in *Gravity's Rainbow.*" In *Mindful Pleasures,* edited by David Leverenz and George Levine, pp. 197–228. Boston: Little, Brown & Co., 1976.

Kolodny, Annette, and Daniel Peters. "Pynchon's *The Crying of Lot 49:* The Novel as Subversive Experience." *Modern Fiction Studies* 19 (spring 1973): 79–87.

Krafft, John. "Anarcho-Romanticism and the Metaphysics of Counterforce: Alex Comfort and Thomas Pynchon." *Paunch* 40–41 (April 1975): 78–107.

———. "And How Far-Fallen: Puritan Themes in *Gravity's Rainbow.*" *Critique* 18, no. 3 (1977): 55–73.

Leland, John. "Pynchon's Linguistic Demon: *The Crying of Lot 49.*" *Critique* 16, no. 2 (1974): 45–53.

Leverenz, David. "On Trying to Read *Gravity's Rainbow.*" In *Mindful Pleasures,* edited by David Leverenz and George Levine, pp. 229–50. Boston: Little, Brown & Co., 1976.

Levine, George. "Risking the Moment: Anarchy and Possibility in Pynchon's Fiction." In *Mindful Pleasures,* edited by David Leverenz and George Levine, pp. 113–36. Boston: Little, Brown & Co., 1976.

———. "V-2." *Partisan Review* 40, no. 3 (1973): 517–29.

Levine, George, and David Leverenz. "Introduction: Mindful Pleasures." *Twentieth Century Literature* 21 (May 1975): iii–v.

LeVot, André. "The Rocket and the Pig: Thomas Pynchon and Science Fiction." *Caliban XII* 11 (1975); 111–18.

Lewis, R. W. B. *Trials of the Word.* New Haven: Yale University Press, 1965.

Lhamon, W. T. "The Most Irresponsible Bastard." *New Republic,* 14 April 1973, pp. 24–28.

———. "Pentecost, Promiscuity, and Pynchon's *V.:* From the Scaffold to the Impulsive." *Twentieth Century Literature* 21 (May 1975): 163–76.

Locke, Richard. "*Gravity's Rainbow.*" *New York Times Book Review,* 11 March 1973, pp. 1, 14.

Lyons, Thomas R., and Allan D. Franklin. "Thomas Pynchon's 'Classic' Presentation of the Second Law of Thermodynamics." *Bulletin of the Rocky Mountain Modern Language Association* 27 (1973): 195–204.

Maddocks, Melvin. "Paleface Takeover." *Atlantic Monthly,* March 1973, pp. 98–101.

Mangel, Anna. "Maxwell's Demon, Entropy, Information: *The Crying of Lot 49.*" *Tri-Quarterly* 20 (1971): 194–208.

Mendelson, Edward. "Gravity's Encyclopedia." In *Mindful Pleasures*, edited by David Leverenz and George Levine, Boston: Little, Brown & Co., 1976.
———. "Pynchon's Gravity." *Yale Review* 62 (summer 1973): 624–31.
———. "Rainbow Corner." *Times Literary Supplement*, 13 June 1975, p. 666.
———. "The Sacred, the Profane, and *The Crying of Lot 49*." In *Individual and Community: Variations on a Theme in American Fiction*, edited by Kenneth Baldwin and David Kirby. Durham, N. C.: Duke University Press, 1975, 182–222.
Morrison, Philip. "Books." *Scientific American*, October 1973, p. 131.
Nash, James W. "Chaos, Structure and Salvation in the Novels of Thomas Pynchon." Dissertation, University of Houston, 1974.
Olderman, Raymond. *Beyond the Wasteland: The American Novel in the Nineteen-Sixties*. New Haven: Yale University Press, 1972.
Ozier, Lance. "Antipointsman/Antimexico: Some Mathematical Imagery in *Gravity's Rainbow*." *Critique* 16, no. 2 (1974): 73–89.
———. "The Calculus of Transformation: More Mathematical Imagery in *Gravity's Rainbow*." *Twentieth Century Literature* 21 (May 1975): 193–210.
Patteson, Richard. "What Stencil Knew: Structure and Certitude in Pynchon's *V*." *Critique* 16, no. 2 (1974): 30–43.
Poirier, Richard. "Cook's Tour." *New York Review of Books* 2 (1963): 52.
———. "The Importance of Thomas Pynchon." *Twentieth Century Literature* 21 (May 1975): 151–62.
———. "Rocket Power." *Saturday Review of the Arts* 1 (March 1973): 59–64.
Robinson, David. "Unaccommodated Man: The Estranged World in Contemporary Fiction: Nathanael West, Joseph Heller, and Thomas Pynchon." Dissertation, Duke University 1971.
Rovit, Earl. "Some Shapes in Recent American Fiction." *Contemporary Literature* 15 (summer 1974): 552–53.
Sale, Roger. "American Fiction in 1973." *Massachusetts Review* 14 (autumn 1973): 840–46.
Sanders, Scott. "Pynchon's Paranoid History." *Twentieth Century Literature* 21 (May 1975): 177–92.
Schmitz, Neil. "Describing the Demon: The Appeal of Thomas Pynchon." *Partisan Review* 42 (January 1975), 112–25.
Siegel, Mark. "Creative Paranoia: Understanding the System of *Gravity's Rainbow*." *Critique* 18, no. 3 (1977): 39–54.
Simmon, Scott. "A Character Index: *Gravity's Rainbow*." *Critique* 16, no. 2 (1974): 68–72.
———. "*Gravity's Rainbow* Described." *Critique* 16, no. 2 (1974): 54–67.
Sissman, L. E. "Hieronymus and Robert Bosch: The Art of Thomas Pynchon." *New Yorker*, 19 May 1973, p. 138.
Sklar, Robert. "The New Novel U. S. A.: Thomas Pynchon." *The Nation*, 25 September 1967, pp. 277–80.
Slade, Joseph. "Escaping Rationalization: Options for the Self in *Gravity's Rainbow*." *Critique* 18, no. 3 (1977): 27–38.
———. *Thomas Pynchon*. New York: Warner Paperback Library, 1974.
Sperry, Joseph. "Henry Adams and Thomas Pynchon: The Entropic Movements of Self, Society and Truth." Dissertation, Ohio State University 1974.
Stark, John. "The Arts and Sciences of Thomas Pynchon." *Hollins Critic* 4 (October 1975): 1–13.
Stimpson, Catharine R. "Pre-Apocalyptic Atavism: Thomas Pynchon's Early Fiction." In *Mindful Pleasures*, edited by David Leverenz and George Levine, pp. 31–48. Boston: Little, Brown & Co., 1976.
Storris, Eric. "The Worldly Palimpsest of Thomas Pynchon." *Harper's*, June 1973, pp. 78–82.

Tanner, Tony. *City of Words: American Fiction 1950-1970.* New York: Harper & Row, Publishers, 1971.

Vesterman, William. "Pynchon's Poetry." *Twentieth Century Literature* 21 (May 1975): 211-20.

Weixlmann, Joseph. "Thomas Pynchon: A Bibliography." *Critique* 14, no. 2 (1972): 34-43.

Winston, Mathew. "The Quest for Pynchon." *Twentieth Century Literature* 22 (October 1975): 278-87.

Wood, Michael. "Rocketing to the Apocalypse." *New York Review of Books,* 22 March 1973, pp. 22-23.

Young, James Dean. "The Enigma Variation of Thomas Pynchon." *Critique* 10, no. 1 (1967): 69-77.

INDEX

DATE DUE

NOV 2 0 '79			
NOV 15 '79			
FEB 1 2 '80			
FEB 18 '80			
AUG 1 4 '81			
SEP 3 '84			
DEC 1 0 '85			
DEC 9 '85			
GAYLORD			PRINTED IN U.S.A.